REAL ESTATE

25 BEST STRATEGIES FOR REAL ESTATE INVESTING, HOME BUYING AND FLIPPING HOUSES

TABLE OF CONTENTS

INTRODUCTION

The real estate industry is considered to be one of the most lucrative industries in the world of business, and for good reason. In fact, it is so lucrative that there are countless rags to riches stories of people who went from being an average Joe to multi-millionaire overnight by dabbling in this industry. And there is an equal number of cases where people have lost their life savings and family fortunes in the quest to make money by parlaying in land.

One of the many reasons why so many people are lured into this industry is the fact that, unlike other professions, you do not require any formal higher educational qualifications to deal in real estate. That is not say that it does not require any expertise but anyone with good inter-personal skills and entrepreneurial tact can make it big in this profession. Plus, if you know good tradesmen and can build a team of experts, you can really make a killing on the market.

Not only can it help people turn into millionaires, it can also allow them to buy/ rent the house of their dreams. But as good as it sounds, the art of dealing with properties is said to be a very tough task. The real estate market is seen as being a tough nut to crack, given its obscure nature.

Every year, many people venture into it but give up on it all too soon. People tend to either expect too much or end up making all the wrong moves. Nevertheless, it is the one industry which guarantees a return on investment and allows a certain flexibility, in terms of investment options.

In this book, we look at 25 of the best strategies that you can employ, in order to score the best properties in your town. We explore the various aspects that you need to consider, in order to be able to land the best deals.

The book will also explore the 5 "Don'ts" of the industry, and help you exercise precaution, when you step into the big bad world of real estate.

I want to thank you for buying this book and hope that it helps you understand the property market in a better manner. The property market offers potential for investment for those who are prepared to put in the groundwork. Once you do, you will find that the equity in a home can be increased to such an extent that your work earns you good money.

CHAPTER 1

GETTING STARTED: KNOW WHAT YOU ARE GETTING YOURSELF INTO

Whereas there is no doubt that investment in real estate is usually

a good place to put your money, like other ventures in life, it also

requires due diligence and careful consideration. One of the im-

portant aspects I would like to bring to your attention is the need

to sit still and take a careful view of the area in you wish to localize

your investment. Remember, your investment is not an entity in

isolation but is influenced by several other factors; some of which

are outside your scope of influence. You need to ask yourself sev-

eral questions before you venture into the actual process of invest-

ment. Here are 10 critical questions that will help you follow a safe

path and have an easier time investing in real estate.

What is that structure that is being built?

The structures being constructed close to the location you wish to put your investment (where you want to build a single or multi-family unit or even a commercial structure), may influence your investment either positively or negatively. Sometimes it may not elicit any immediate correlation but soon after you have set up, you begin to see the indirect effects. Therefore, find out what it is and what its purpose is. It may make or break your future business. For instance, a school, a college, or another structure could mean different things to your real estate investment compared to some other investment, say a factory or airport. You need to work out what building works are going on in the area where you are about to invest. If the new works mean an improvement in services that could be good news.

What is the properties' value?

One of the terrible mistakes I have witnessed, especially with those who are newbies in the real estate investment niche is the tendency to take things at face value or for granted. Newbies tend to believe many hearsay stories that agents tell them. However, experience shows that these agents are sellers who are eager to reap the most they can from buyers. Therefore, do not believe everything your agent tells you about the estimated rental returns and other prospects for growth. It is worth your while and money to invest in a property valuer/appraiser. The main reason here is that the selling price is not always the value of the property. There are companies that specialize in valuation of property. Such entities will help you save lots of money. Other benefits you derive from investing in property valuation service include

- You get a chance to use the figures from valuation to negotiate and leverage against high pricing by the sellers.
- You also reduce the risks you are getting into by a significant percentage.
- You get the best price possible for the property. This is because you bargain from a point of knowledge.

The study that you put into this is vital to your investment and having professional appraisers on your side will help you to establish what a property is worth rather than what you are being told it is worth by someone with a vested interest in gaining money from the sale.

What's going on in the local market?

It is important for you to understand the trends in the investment industry. Learning what is going on in the local market can help you determine what prices are fair and which ones are out of whack. Such knowledge may help you make smart decisions such as avoiding to commit when the market is saturated with buyers and investors in the same niche as the one you are interested in. Buying at a time when there are many other competitors exposes you to the risk of overpaying. Overpaying in turn eats into the possible profits you could possibly derive from your investment. Moreover, the snowball effect of falling into such a trap may further leave you financially deprived. If you fail to secure occupancy for your property in good time or even fail to get quality tenants, you may be compromised when it comes to paying for the bank loan you may have taken to finance your investment. Every moment that your property is empty costs you money.

Another benefit of walking around to learn the local markets is that you get to understand other dynamics that influence the demand for the kind of property you invest in. Walking around helps you learn the security situation of the local area. Ask about crime rates. You may want to visit the local authority offices to enquire about the state of security. The demographics of the area will also influence the returns from your investment. You should also know the rate of employment and income capacity of the locals. What kind of people live there? Are houses selling in that area? What kind of rental can you expect to achieve and for what type of accommodation?

What do you stand to gain in rental return?

This critical question is linked directly to your investment goals. Conduct an appraisal for the same. Do not rely solely on what the agent tells you. Look and see what properties are renting for and what people expect to get for their money. The local newspaper will be a good place to look for advertisements.

Are you in the game for a capital return or rental gain?

Note that if you are making multiple investments and your wish is to expand your hold in the industry fast, you need to focus on capital gain. Focusing on rental return is good and may help you finance back your loans but you will remain a sitting duck for a long time as far as expansion is concerned. Capital returns help you acquire other properties fast. It is always a good idea to aim at buying other investments to expand your possibilities for business growth. This is important if you are investing with a strong focus on making more money as soon as possible. Thus decide if you are in the market for buying and doing up houses for sale, or if you have sufficient funds to buy long term investments such as rentals.

What's the competition like?

If you wish to invest in real estate, it is always a great idea to invest in raw markets that have not yet attracted too many investors in the same categories as you. Too many investors in the same niche diminishes your chances of fetching significant rental return from your investment. Moreover, you may end up paying more than the investment can actually return in good time to help you to keep afloat. You should be wary of large apartments in the area. You should also find out the percentage of houses, which are owner-occupied in the area. This helps you decide the type of real estate investment that is suitable for the area. You get to know what is in excess supply and what is really needed. Avoid overused rental locations.

What's written in the property title search results?

This can be a real catch, and indeed many newbies soon find themselves in trouble because they assume that what they see is what they get. Real estate investment has its own share of inner secrets, which a new investor must be privy to in order to make smart investment decisions.

a) Be sure to check what's up for sale and what's not. In this regard, you need to check for such aspects as parking spaces and storage facilities. Some owners fail to update their property details. These can cost you a great deal, if you do not ensure that they are all included in your purchase contract.

b) Look out for any encumbrances on the property

a. What is the state of the property and what repairs need doing?

b. What rights of way are there that affect the property?

c) Check for monthly maintenance status- Some properties set up a sinking fund from which maintenance of the property is funded. These funds are used to conduct such things as painting, fixing electric faults, plumbing repairs, maintaining lifts etc. If you are buying an apartment in a block you will have monthly communal charges to pay so you need to know what they are.

d) Scrutinize to see if the funds available in your accounts are sufficient for the repairs needed. You are going to need to do clever math.

a. Who are you targeting with your investment?- Check the kind of clientele you are likely to get in your rental investment if that's what you want to venture into. If it is located near a university, for example, you need to ensure that the property serves students with convenience. It should be close to the transport system and other amenities such as shopping malls and recreational facilities.

In addition, if your property is near a university, as a property investor, you are likely to gain more if you invest in multiple occupancy property.

If, on the other hand, you want family property, seek a large home with expansive spaces, gardens and open lawns in a safe neighborhood with good schooling.

To what extent do you have to work up the property?

This question relates to the amount of money and time you are likely to spend in repairs. Always ensure that you purchase property that needs minimal repairs. If anything, go for one that is ready to let out. If you opt for one that needs a significant amount of repairs, it may cost you more money as it will cost you money for each month that you have the property vacant. The only thing to be aware of is that if the property is ready to let out, are you paying for the repairs that the owner has done by paying a price that is excessive? Sometimes, you can get bargains that only need superficial repairs and these are the ones to look for.

If you must take one that needs repairs, accept one that only needs minimal and cosmetic fixes such as repainting and refurnishing. Avoid homes that require structural repairs unless of course you have the workforce in place to do these repairs. These will definitely prove costlier in terms of time and money. You will definitely take longer to spruce them up to the level that allows you to rent the property out. The implication is that you will have lost several months and every month the house is empty costs you money.

After you've clearly understood what it is you are getting yourself into, you have to learn the ropes for getting started. As you do that, you have to know the options available to you as an investor. In the next chapter, we will look into these niches to help you make an informed decision. Bear in mind also that only you know what you can afford and the amount of money that you can afford has to include a contingency for the repairs that are needed on the property to make it ready for the market.

CHAPTER 2

REAL ESTATE INVESTMENT NICHES

There are two driving forces when it comes to starting your ideal real estate investment

    i.   You need to how you intend to make your money from your investment

    ii.   How you will reach your goals and keep within your budget

For example, will you be selling or will you be renting. If selling, is there a ready market for what you are offering? If renting, are the rental amounts within that given geographical area worthwhile?

Indeed, there are many choices in real estate investment. The essence of these choices is that they provide anyone interested to fit in with the market available by selecting the option they prefer and one that works in their situation. This means that before you throw in your money blindly, you must conduct a self-assessment and match your finding with the available options in order to select the investment that works in your circumstances. It is necessary, as a starter investor in real estate, to ensure that you tread carefully. Real estate involves colossal sums of money. This means that you cannot afford to lose the money you put in. Experience shows that for you to succeed in real estate, your best bet lies in learning to grow a step at a time. It is a prudent move to choose a niche and learn about it thoroughly before you start.

- Start off with learning. Once you have learnt how the waves flow in the selected niche, you need to start networking. It is hard to succeed in real estate investment without networks. It is such networks that keep you informed of new developments. It is also from such networks that you easily get access to people with different skills; from realtors, to lawyers and repair experts. Use these experts to give you the information that you need to succeed and have your questions ready for them.

- Once you establish the networks, you need to draw a plan of action. Like everything else, you need to plan to have a good chance of succeeding. Discuss this plan of action with experts and see what their reactions are. Take note of their advice. It will be valuable to you.

- Once your plan is in place, then it is time to execute the plan.

The processes mentioned above are much more intricate than highlighted. We shall discuss them in later chapters. Let's have a look at the real estate investment niches at your disposal and have a short discussion on the dynamics that surround them.

Raw Land

Raw land is one of the options you have as a real estate investment option. Raw land presents you with several possibilities for making profit. It is also a flexible option since you can manipulate it and diversify your markets. Raw land presents the following in a nutshell.

- It can be leased or rented cheaply since it's yours. Therefore, what's your market like for this type of land? What is the potential profit?

- It can also be subdivided and sold off at a profit. In fact, this is one of the most attractive aspects of investing in raw land. The economies of scale work in your favor if you can acquire a large piece of raw land and subdivide

it for sale. The law of diminishing returns and economies of scale dictate that if you purchase a large piece
of land and resell it subdivided, you are likely to gain a
lot more because the price of the smaller pieces is com-
paratively higher than similar units as part of the larger
parcel bought as one. How much land does the law dictate should be used for each plot? Is there access to public services? You need to work out your plan and it's
best to know what use that land is allotted to before you
buy it. It may not be used for residential properties and
that really could restrict what you can do with it.

- You can also buy and hold the land, then resell it at a
  profit, if prospects show that there is likely to be a rise
  in prices. Amenities and infrastructural developments in
  the area are often strong indicators for such eventuality.
  If there is a freeway development or an expanding town
  or city nearby, it is best then to buy and hold such land.
  You will soon resell it at a gain. Be careful with your
  choices because this can backfire and your money will
  stay tied up for a while which may make your returns
  restrictive.

Single Family Home

Single-family homes are touted as the easier start offs for newcomers in the real estate investment niche. One of the reasons for this is that they are relatively easier to rent out and require minimal care and attention from you. Single-family units are also easier to sell. Therefore, they can provide near ready equity whenever you need liquid cash. However, you do need to examine the condition and know your market well because if your property is not as good as the competition, it won't sell or rent out. People want value for their investments so you need to be sure that you provide them with the best you can within that given market.

Duplex, triplex and quads

- These are similar to single-family units. The only difference is that they are several such units lumped together. They are usually built attached to each other. They are basically multifamily units and range from 2 to 4 units in a single set. There are advantages and disadvantages to this type of property.

- The advantage with this type of housing unit is that you are exposed to less competition as compared to single-family ones. The reason is obvious. Apart from the fact that they are not exactly an attraction for large real estate investors, they are relatively beyond the reach of most people with middle income.

- These units are a great option for real estate investment especially if you can raise a substantial amount of financing. You gain the advantage of securing financing on similar terms as with single-family units. Most banks and other financing institutions tend to treat these units from the same financial perspective. Therefore, if you take advantage of this, you are likely to gain the advantage of greater rental returns on the same terms as you would get for a single-family unit. Make sure you know what the rules are concerning this type of unit since they may be restrictive especially when it comes to letting.

- These units also stand out as a great investment option because they can be used as personal residence for the investor even as they are rented out to others. This option could also save you money, in terms of rent but equally important, you will be able to oversee the maintenance of your investment from close quarters.

You do not need the services of a property manager unless you are extremely busy or the units are so many that it takes too much time to manage. You also need to assess what the costs will be to each unit to have services which are there for all tenants and owners.

Small Apartments

By market standards, small apartments are the ones that range from 5 to 50 units. 50 is the unwritten drawing line between small and large apartments. Here are the facts about this type of real estate investment option.

- They are a little harder to finance than single family, duplex, triplex or quad types. They can only use commercial lending criteria. This is a more expensive option compared to the lending possibility for single-family units.

- Although financing presents challenges, they are good investments because they give you back greater returns and a steady and stable cash flow. This in turn enables you to reinvest further. This is particularly so if you choose the location in an area where there is a constant need for accommodation.

- They require more astute management plans. Otherwise, they may turn into a liability. Rent collection and repairs must be coordinated if you wish to keep the cash flowing. If you do employ an agency to do this for you, it will cost you a percentage of your income.

- Competition is relatively lower with this investment option. Small apartments are considered too small for the large investors and rather unaffordable for small investors. This also means that there are relatively fewer on the market. However, you can use this to your advantage, especially if you have large companies that are looking for short term accommodation and your accommodation is tailored to their needs.

- The prices for this kind of residential setups are not determined by comparisons. Rather, they are a function of the revenue they are bound to generate. This is an advantage over other options because as an investor, you have something of a blank check. You can play around with the psychological perceptions of tenants by sprucing it up and increasing rental potential. You can reduce expenses, increase rent, and establish better management. This kind of property will often call for engaging an onsite manager to ensure that your property is kept attractive and well maintained. Since there are several housing possibilities, such a manager may be contracted by smartly exchanging their services with housing offer or free. Thus, with the right deal struck with a manager who is conscientious, you are likely to have very happy tenants.

Large Apartments

These kinds of housing units are the up-market options. They are the ones that come with a range of other services such as pools and wellness centers. They also come with full time staff and large advertising budgets. The following characteristics are commonly associated with large apartment establishments.

- They are relatively more expensive. They require millions of dollars to build.

- They also yield huge amounts of returns. This is a direct result of the economies of scale. If there are sufficient units; each generates a potential rental income.

- These investments require highly reduced personal input. They are commonly set up by groups of people who pool their resources and engage property managers to execute transactions on their behalf. These are also great when they are located in areas where holiday lettings are popular because you can refurbish and offer them through websites that deal with travel.

REITs

This is shorthand for Real Estate Investment Trust. This is similar to investing in mutual funds in stocks. For REITs, investors pool their financial resources and form a REIT. They, in turn, commission the REIT to transact on their behalf. The REIT purchases and sells property in the interest of the members. REITs deal in large properties. They are the ones usually responsible for the large shopping malls in towns and cities. Other ventures that REITs often pursue include:

- Large apartment blocks

- Numerous units of single-family apartments, duplexes, and triples. Some of the acquisitions go into hundreds

- Skyscrapers

Some Facts about REITs

- Although REITs generate colossal amounts of revenue from the large investments that are made, the returns are not usually as handsome as you would get from a single-family unit or small apartment house because REITs are often owned by a large number of people who share out the profits. The profits are spread out to members on an equitable basis. Thus if you choose this route, you can expect to have minimal profits but perhaps long term security.

- They are a great real estate investment opportunity because they are the most hands-off ownerships in the real estate investment market. The only things you are required to do is buy your shares in a group and provide your account. You can go about your other commitments leaving the work to others. The relatively lower returns you get are compensated with the freedom to pursue other ventures. This means that these investments are worth considering by people who want to place funds in a secure place for future security, rather than being dependent upon a quick return.

- The public can access shares in REITs through the regular stocks and investments platforms such as stock exchanges. Even though the returns from REITs are relatively lower compared to direct involvement in productive real estate ventures, their dividends are still by far higher than most other stocks return. For those who have money to invest but who are not manual in their skills, this is probably a very good sound investment.

Commercial Properties

This category exhibits a large variance in terms of size, purpose location, style and income. The bottom-line is that commercial properties have to do with renting out or leasing property for business operations by others. For properties of this nature, they need prime locations where businesses can maximize their potential.

The question as to whom you can lease or rent your property to is a matter of personal judgment, market dynamics, and sometimes, local legislation requirements. For example, there may be local rules concerning the sale of alcohol or the change of use of such a property and that is something you need to ascertain before you invest, to save disappointment. Things that will be borne in mind are availability for clients to park, other businesses in the area and the need for such a business venture.

Here are some facts about commercial properties

- They have a good promise for consistent cash flow because businesses pay regularly

- You risk longer holding time spans in between leases and rent periods because businesses are much more reliable than tenants

- They are often held for long periods by tenants who represent companies rather than individuals

- Investment in commercial properties isn't a beginner's cup of tea. It requires shrewdness and experience. It also requires a significant level of stability to cover for the many possible risks. You need to know your market.

Mobile Homes

Mobile homes are an increasingly popular variety of housing in the USA.

The facts

- It is possible to invest in this niche with money straight out of your pocket because they are relatively cheap investments. This type is especially ideal for foreigners who might find it hard to access loan facilities in banks.

- They do not have as much return as you would get from other conventional methods but the secret lies in numbers; the more you have, the more you are likely to generate decent income.

- Most of the strategies used in the other methods still work perfectly well with mobile homes.

- The thing that you need to think of it what you can offer overall. Will your trailer park have security? Will there be facilities that tenants can enjoy? Is it in an area which is popular for those who have to go to work every day? Can you sustain the level of upkeep that you promise at the outset?

XI. Notes

Notes are basically paper mortgages with value.

When buying property on loan, a note detailing the terms of purchase is usually crafted. If the original owner offers it for 2 million dollars for instance, he may decide to carry the note. In the process, they will have circumvented the typical need for clients to use a bank as the platform for their transactions. If the buyer is to pay for the mortgage at an interest rate of 10% over 30 years until 2 million dollars is paid up plus the interest due, the original owner may hold on to the note, continue to collect the premiums and installments or still take the liberty to sell off the note to another owner at a discounted rate. The new owner then proceeds to collect the payments until the original selling price is fulfilled and all the interest due is paid up as agreed in the terms.

The sale of the original property may continue until the property is fully paid up by the long-term buyer.

Summary of Real Estate Investment Niches

It is evident from the above that the options for investment in real estate are many and spread out financially and geographically. These factors present different opportunities to different people in different ways. The niches are investment vehicles, which you need to choose and ride to your destination. For example, if you have a mortgage on a property and are able to recuperate the mortgage payments in the way of rent, your mortgage is paid for you, but you retain the real estate value of the property which was rented.

Now that you have some background information about the available investing options, we will now go into details about the strategies to follow while investing in real estate. We will start with the most basic ones. To get started, we will discuss some 5 important strategies that you need to follow as you get started.

Choosing a Niche

Although the possibilities above may seem endless, they are just hypothetical until you choose the niche that works for you. Failing to lock in on your target is just as good as not knowing that there are niches. So how do you choose your niche? Let's discuss this briefly.

For you to identify an ideal niche, you need to know the different real estate investment options at your disposal. You cannot specialize on a niche when you don't know what else is available. Identifying a niche is the first step to ensuring that you use effective marketing campaigns for your property. Additionally, when you know your niche, it is easy to specialize on that niche and become an expert at it as opposed to selling anything that comes your way. For you to narrow down on a niche, you should answer the following question first:

Who are your targeted customers? And what are the specific characteristics of these customers? You can check the customer persona guide here to help narrow down your search.

After you identify your customer, you should then ask yourself the type of service that your target customer is looking for. After you do that, you should then proceed to ask yourself what it is you can do to attract, nurture, retain and service that ideal customer. For example, if you buy a home in a family neighborhood, then your obvious customer base would be families. You need to know your niche because that helps you to prepare the property to fit the niche in question.

After you've identified your niche, it is very critical that you invest in making sure that the niche is consistent with the market. For instance, if your target customers are first time homebuyers, you should then do your research to identify stats and figures that back up your idea that the niche is viable in that market. For instance, find out the percentage of sales within your target market who were first time buyers within the last 12-16 months, and how much was the price of these homes? You should also assess the level of competition in this market. Will you be the only person catering for that niche or are there others who are already established? Be very specific when discussing this in your business plan to iron out all the details concerning your potential market then explain how you would be able to make your properties stand out even with the competition that exists. For this to be possible, you need to do a SWOT analysis to help you take advantage of your strengths, deal with weaknesses, and identify opportunities and fight off any threats. You need to come up with a list of each i.e. a list of strengths, a list of weaknesses, list of opportunities, and a list of threats in your market. Listing at least 5 things is a good idea. The kind of things that I mean are the types of properties, the competition – the price range of these properties, the cost of investment and repair before the property can be sold on at a profit. You also need to know whether the area is a developing area and whether changes are taking place in the market that could enhance the potential price of housing. This is something that's easy to find out. If you find that refurbishments are being made in an area which would normally be considered below par, that's a good sign that the area is going to have demand for housing, if the area is improved.

Note: You need to outline everything clearly in a business plan if you really want your execution of every activity to be nicely structured. You can refer to the ideas at the end of this book on how to prepare a business plan for your real estate business.

CHAPTER 3

THE 5 MAIN STRATEGIES TO GET YOU STARTED

When I started writing the book, my main aim was to explain to you a thing or two about scoring the best deals in the real estate industry. I hope by the end of it, the cause is justified. The book is divided into 5 main chapters, where each one will explore a certain aspect of the industry. In this chapter, we look at the 5 main strategies that you will need to employ in order to make the right decision in terms of buying/ selling and renting a place out at a profit.

Strategy 1: Bargain Like Your Life Depends on it

The first and most important strategy in the world of real estate is to bargain like crazy. Buying a property can be a very expensive deal and most sellers will have cranked up the prices, just to allow the buyer a little leeway to conduct his/ her bargaining. So no matter how desperate you are to score a particular property, never buy it at the going price. There is always room for leverage. This can depend on various things. The state of repair of the property can be used as bargaining power.

Start by conducting a bit of research around the area and arriving at a price that you think would be ideal for a property in that particular area. The way to do this is to look at properties which are for sale in the same area and which offer the same kind of accommodation. You also need to see how the market is shifting in the area where you are investing. If there is a glut of property, are you likely to be able to sell? Speak to real estate agencies and see what the market is like and how fast houses are moving because otherwise, you could end up with a white elephant. What you also need to know is the price of properties in that area and whether the home in question needs to be updated in any way to meet other houses being offered at a similar price. Sellers often put a price on their homes with the hope that they will achieve that price and very near it. However, people get attached to houses and there are several indications that you may get a reduction.

If a property has been for sale for any length of time, then chances are that the seller will be glad to get a certain sale at a lower price and this is a good indication that you do have leverage to bring your offer down substantially from the price advertised.

Another thing which will help you is if the property needs repairs. It makes the house less valuable and you can also use this to substantiate a drop in the offer you are prepared to make. Remember, if your repair estimates put the price above the market value of the house, you are not likely to make a profit. Thus if the seller is not prepared to adjust his price, learn to walk away. There are always other houses on the market.

Start by quoting 10% less than what you actually plan to pay for it. Do not assume that the buyer will accept it and do it with confidence, explaining the disadvantages or the list of repairs that you have to make to break even. The other party will try to raise it and you can then quote 5% below your price. Ultimately, you will get to pay exactly what you wish to and the seller will be forced to compromise. It does not always work, but the tactic should be to put together this equation:

- What can I afford to spend in total for the house and for the renovations?
- Take away the price of the house.
- Is it viable that a profit can be made?

For example, if you buy a home at $150,000 and know that your repairs are going to cost you $50,000 to bring the house up to a standard to sell easily, is the asking price likely to be realistic at $200,000? If it isn't, then offering that much isn't viable. Another way you can look at this is if you are considering buying to make the property into rental units. How much will a mortgage cost you per month? Will the rental you can charge on each unit add up to enough to pay the mortgage? When you do invest in properties for rental, the way to recoup the cost is to make sure that the rental you want to charge is viable in that area and a friendly real estate agent will be able to tell you what people expect to pay for what you are offering. The mistake people often make is paying too high a price, doing the house up to modern specs and then finding that the rentals that they can achieve are less than the mortgage costs. If this is the case, you need to offer a lower price.

Remember, money is valuable to everyone. The person with whom you are dealing with also acts with the intention of deriving maximum for the money he has spent. Hence, he will come to the table with as much fervor as you to draw a profit from the transaction.

And you do not even have to be buying it for the keeps. Even if you plan on flipping it, you have to quote your exact budget and do not budge. You can never be under prepared, as the seller might have several tricks up his sleeve, which might baffle and fool you and prevent you from being able to bargain to your best advantage.

You should always make sure at the time of making an offer that you have evaluated the property in comparison with similar houses in the area and that you have estimated in as accurate a manner as possible the following remedial works:

- Wiring

- Plumbing

- Kitchen refurbishment

- Other repairs including dampness and underpinning (these are expensive)

Remember that the work that you do has reach code and it's a good idea to look around the house for indications as to whether the house has been well maintained or not. There are usually tell-tale signs that a house needs loving care because the owner will have left jobs undone and you will also notice that there are many things which he should have tackled before even putting the house on the market. These can indicate that a house has been neglected and may spell more costs once you start stripping the place down. Thus the price that you offer has to take all of this into account.

Strategy 2: Understand and Undertake "Flipping"

"Flipping" is a very common and popular real estate practice and is one of the newer forms of practice. The practice entails you buying a particular property and selling it almost immediately. You need not even wait to completely own the house and can simultaneously sell it off.

The idea is to sell the house for a profit and so it will be important to look for lucrative deals. You will have to hunt for a house that is in good condition and the seller is pricing it at a rate that is below the trending price. Flipping which is more responsible involves buying a fixer-upper and then fixing it up so that it realizes a better price. This is common since programs like the Property Brothers have hit prime time television. They show the whole process of giving clients a dream home at a price that they can afford and flipping houses achieves this. You buy, you refurbish and you sell.

The main advantage of the first process is that you do not have to spend too much time pondering over the renovation aspect of a place. You can sell it as it is and avoid incurring any additional costs. The advantage of the second process is that you do sell a home that is in great condition and realize a much better price.

But bear in mind that you cannot rent the property out and you have to sell it outright if you want to make money from flipping. If, on the other hand, you want to make long-term investment, you can rent it, but be sure that the housing market in the area where the house is located needs rental properties and for whom they are needed. For example, providing family accommodation in an executive uptown area may not be the best way to go. Find out who rents property in the area in question because all of the work that you do to the house will need to be geared to that market. Markets are shown here which are potentially good for rent:

- Is there a local university that needs extra accommodation for students?

- Are there a lot of businesses that want executive accommodation for visitors?

- Is this an area where there isn't enough rental accommodation for families?

This type of a deal can help you make profits at an elevated pace and the dangers of incurring losses can be cut down to size. Most house flippers prefer to resell at a profit of 10-15% and as per a 2012 study concluded; a gross average of $30,000 is the standard profit margin for most flipped houses. However, would you prefer to buy and hold the property, knowing that the rental market within the area is likely to pay you enough so that you have a steady cash flow to meet the price of a mortgage loan?

The average ball park price of a $100,000 mortgage, depending upon the term of the mortgage, can be as much as $600 a month, so you need to clear much more than this to cover the mortgage and to gain regular income from renting the house. Check with your bank for the current bank rates, as these will vary depending upon the timescale in which you are asking and the area in which you live.

Strategy 3: Know When to "Buy and Hold"

The next type of a deal is for you to buy a property and hold it. This is very different from flipping, as it does not involve any immediate reselling.

With a buy and hold strategy, you can wait for its value to increase. You are not required to rush into looking for potential buyers and so you can wait for the profit margin to increase beyond 15%. Don't assume that this will happen overnight. It won't. If you are going to buy a property to hold onto, you also need to be aware that you need to present it eventually in a renovated state so that people know what they are getting for their money.

This may be in an upcoming area where you know that prices are rising. The best way to establish this is to look for areas where modernization is happening. At the moment, the houses may have a small value, but clues will exist that the market is going up. Look for skips and professional renovations going on in the area. The area may be one that is not vibrant at this time, but one that is becoming more fashionable. I always look to see what activity is going on in an area because being informed about the area helps you to know which run down areas are being refurbished and once the market is more buoyant, you can sell at a very good profit.

With buy and hold, you have all the time in the world to renovate the place and help increase its value. However, it's not wise to wait too long. Perhaps you can fit this between other jobs. The reason why you shouldn't leave renovations too long is that the cost of both your workforce and materials is always on the increase. So your initial investment needs to be small and you must expressly look for houses that are undervalued. This is a very lucrative proposition if done properly. There will be many properties that are under-valued on the market, but which have the potential to increase exponentially in value if some renovation is carried.

And more often than not, you will end up making a very tidy profit over and above the purchase price of the property plus the amount spent on renovation and restoration.

This may apply to houses that are sold off at auction, but you will need to have the money ready to put down on the house on the auction day. These are typically houses that have been repossessed by lenders because the owner could not keep up with payments on their mortgage. All they are interested in is getting their money back, so they are often sold at prices, which are very attractive to property developers. Decide on the price that the house is worth before you go to an auction, as newbies at this tend to be very carried away with their bidding. Decide on your maximum and never go over it in the excitement of the moment. It's a very foolish thing to do and you may find yourself breaking even or even losing money if you let you bidding get too high.

This type, in fact, is said to help rake in huge profits as the value of a property always increases, but you have to make sure that there are no bigger developers interested in the property because the competition will be tough. They can afford to offer a little more because they already have their own tradesmen and contacts in the trade for buying all the necessary replacement items for the house and you don't. If you find that developers are bidding too high, walk away.

So the best places to invest in buy and hold properties are at upcoming and developing localities. Once it develops completely, your property will grow in value and you will be able to make a big profit out of it. The thing to watch out here is bigger properties with more availability of funds. You can still snap up bargains, and it's worthwhile looking at all properties which are being sold because of repossession since these offer you a much higher possibility long term and may be worthwhile holding as part of your portfolio until the area is fully developed and the prices have risen sufficiently highly to make a big profit.

The buy and hold investment strategy is a straightforward approach in real estate, yet it is the straightforwardness that should stir you to think radically. The so-called straightforward process can actually lead straight to a furnace that burns your money; straightforward. In buying and holding, there are ideally two practical executions:

a) Buying property and renting it out or leasing

b) Buying and holding on to your property until such time that the market signals better returns, then you sell.

One advantage with the latter approach is that mortgage is paid every month, thus decreasing the principal balance. This in turn increases your equity in the investment.

Important elements to consider in the buy and hold strategy

You need to understand the process of evaluation of real estate as this is for ever changing. Some of the pitfalls that await the new-bies in real estate buy and hold strategy include

- Underestimation of expenses

- Poor tenant selection

- Poor management

Your solution to the above problems lies in education. You need to educate yourself sufficiently before you commit your hard-earned money in real estate property. If you don't learn the ropes and the details beforehand, you will learn the hard way. This means you are likely to lose money and time. Sometimes it may even cost you freedom. Remember real estate is a highly regulated business in most countries across the globe.

One critical lesson you must hold close to your heart in the buy and hold strategy is that you should never close in for a purchase at a time everybody else is buying. When you get excited about a property targeted by many possible buyers, you are likely to compete for it and push the price up, often beyond levels that make business sense in investment terms.

Conversely, it is also prudent to hold on to your property and avoid selling it, if the markets drop. It may be just as prudent to pay off the mortgage and wait for a sunny day. In the meantime, you can opt for renting or leasing and maintain a steady cash flow. When there is excess demand for a particular type of property, and the players move in to close purchases, the market soon suffers effects of surge and transfers the negative effects to the same property owners. The property you held during a low storm may fetch you a fortune if you are patient enough.

Strategy 4: Hybrid

You can also make reasonable money from combining the benefits of flipping and the long-term benefits of holding. Buy property during low market times, hold it, and resell when the season is favorable. In this form of a strategy, you can buy a property and renovate it before renting it out. This approach can also be used to maximize on ROI and check the risks involved. There are many ways you can establish some cash flow during times when you are holding property.

You can rent it for a certain period, say, until you recover all your expenses and then sell it at a high price.

That way, not only do you get to renovate the place for free, you also get to make a huge profit. This is a good bet if you are in an area where there is a home shortage. Often, this is the case where there are rental properties and once you have finished letting and your tenants have paid you sufficiently to recoup your costs, you can tidy the place up ready to sell at the then going rate.

So look for houses that require a fair bit of renovation and decide to go hybrid with it. You must also have insight and only invest in those that are better and look good after a renovation.

But make sure that you prepare a clause in the rent deed, where you particularly mention the current occupant paying for the renovation charges (if any) after they are made to vacate. This is usually done as part of the rental agreement and a deposit is usually held by your agent to make up for any damage which is done during the occupation by the tenant. However, if you are knocking residential property into a few rental units, you need to be aware that you will sell the property better if reconverted back into one dwelling. Thus any alterations that you make for renting the property should bear this in mind and make the conversion back to one dwelling as straightforward as possible.

It's always best to plan ahead if you think that you might want to sell the property after it has been rented out. Those who are shortsighted and try to sell a property after tenants often find that the property doesn't fit well with the buying market and is more suited to tenants. Thus, your architect or your plans should allow for the potential of easily converting the property back into one dwelling at the time you decide the market is buoyant enough to sell.

Strategy 5: The wonders of Sub-letting

Sub-letting is the other option that you can consider, when you wish to invest in real estate. In sub-letting, you can acquire a property on a lease or a rent basis and then sublet it at a higher rate.

When you do so, you have to make sure that you treat it as a commercial outlet. For example: if you rent a condo, you have to try and convert it into a bachelor pad and allow a lot of visitors to stay. That way, you get to make a huge amount of profit, as the difference in rent paid and rent received will be big.

To try to explain this a little better, sometimes you can rent or take up lease options on a property, which is in a touristic area. The subletting would be at vacation rents rather than rental that local people would expect to pay so there is the potential to make more money. Watch out for service charges. In a property suitable to rent out as a bachelor pad or a holiday let, you are likely to have to pay charges for communal areas or for the upkeep of communal amenities such as swimming pool, corridors, lifts and gardens. Be sure of what your lease includes and check whether you are permitted to sublet. There may be restrictions in some geographical areas prohibiting you from subletting.

You can simultaneously sublet a lot of houses and even entire buildings for that matter, and help garner a huge profit if this is permitted. This is a fairly good long term plan because it means that you are increasing the value of your portfolio of properties all the time and can use the funds that you receive as profits toward future projects.

Bonus: The Sandwich Lease Option

This option offers you a chance to control property at a given price for a given period. You can then resell the lease at a profit. Ideally, it allows you to subcontract with another lease with new terms that are only applicable to you and the new lease owner. This arrangement also makes you enjoy the benefits of a middleman.

In this chapter, we have detailed the different types of property transaction, which are of interest to those who want to start flipping houses. Don't believe that every home has the potential for profit. Some can eat up your contingency funds very rapidly if you don't inspect them properly, as under the walls or dry walling, there may be a nightmare of remedial work which will need to be done. As the modern concept is open plan living, it's quite likely that you will strip a property and may even take down internal walls to give the home that open plan feel that people like. While you may want to change the configuration of the home as well, be aware that moving anything like bathrooms and water outlets may turn out to be costly, if you don't work with existing outlets and use that as a guide as to where new bathrooms should be located. For example, placing a bathroom on the side of the house that has no drainage may mean a lot more work because you need to run pipes through areas that are currently devoid of pipes. All of this has to be considered when you are buying a house. These kinds of alterations affect the profit margins considerably.

Think about each type of investment when you go into flipping houses but don't assume there is one rule for all houses. There isn't. The kind of market that is available in the area where you make the purchase is what matters. You cannot create a new market. You need to know that you are targeting the kind of market you are aiming for and that this kind of buyer will be interested in the area. If you decide to opt for renting a property, you also need to know whether the area lends itself to lets and whether there is a glut of rental property in the area, because this cuts down the amount of chance you have of successfully renting the home.

The longer a house takes to renovate and move on, the more it will cost you. Each month is valuable time and money because while you are responsible for the house, you have all the housing taxes to pay and the household bills. Thus, your planning should be timed in such a way as to minimize the length of time that the house will empty because empty houses cost you money.

CHAPTER 4

THE LOCATION

In the previous chapter, we looked at the various types of property dealings that you can make when you decide to invest in real estate. In this one, we look at the various aspects of a property that you must consider, in order to land the best and most lucrative ones.

Strategy 6: Location, location, location!

The location is the first thing that you will have to bear in mind when you go property or house hunting. Even if you do not wish to stay in the place that you buy, you have to carefully consider the location. The reason for this is that it will:

   i.   Determine price

   ii.   Determine the market available in that area

   iii.   It will determine the kind of profit to be made

The problem with looking in an area you are unfamiliar with is that you don't know the price structure for that area, so you do need to do your homework. What looks cheap to you may be expensive for that area.

Within a couple of miles, house prices can vary considerably. We said in the previous chapter that you need to compare the house with what else in on the market and how much the market is moving. Say, for example, you buy a house a little overpriced and renovate it and then find that the market in that particular area isn't that good at the moment. You may be left with a house on your hands that you can't get rid of.

Know your market. Do your homework and check up on houses, which are similar within that geographical area. Don't take for granted that just because there are certain prices shown in newspaper advertisements that those prices will be realized. Talk to real estate agents and find out whether people are actually getting good prices and how much the market is moving. Also find out what kind of people are buying in the area because then you know whether you are targeting family use, students or business people. You may even be targeting first time buyers. You need to know before you refurbish because it makes a difference to the renovation that you envision.

When you look for a property, make sure that it is located in a reasonably desirable area. It does not always have to be sea facing or have mountains in the background, but just a shady avenue or one with an impressive porch will do the trick. The point is that when you market the property, you need it to look attractive. If you buy a house in a run-down area and renovate it, is it likely to put off potential purchasers? Would it put you off buying the home? If it would, you are looking at the wrong house to flip. The whole premise of flipping houses depends upon swift turnover; so buying a house in an undesirable area is a mistake, unless you are prepared to hold onto it until the area becomes more upmarket.

You must also consider the neighborhood and do a research of the type of people who surround the property. The thing is that families will want different things to single people. Renters will want different things depending upon who they are. For example, business renters will want upmarket accommodation that suits their status, while families will be more inclined to buy a home with a garden in an area, which offers good schooling.

Basic amenities such as supermarkets, malls, hospitals, schools and offices also need to be at close proximity, in order for you to successfully flip or sublet a property. Know your market from the outset because then you know what kind of refit you are going to have to do to attract the right kind of buyers.

And when you wish to stay at a particular location, you must make sure that you are surrounded by relatives and friends otherwise you will struggle to live in a house, even if it is the one from your dreams. Thus, you need to look at the kind of people who live in the area where you are looking at a house, because these are the types of people you will be marketing to.

Family accommodation may need sufficient bedrooms for kids and a large kitchen and family room, whereas an executive apartment or house may look slick and more bachelor friendly. That's why you need to know your market. The house needs to be refurbished to suit the type of people you are marketing. Business people are likely to want space and en suite bathrooms and dressing rooms, whereas families are more interested in how the house works for a family dwelling and would look at practicalities.

Strategy 7: Price Consideration

The price should be your second consideration. Often, people end up over-paying for a property, just because they have the resources to invest. But even if you are a millionaire, you have to consider doing research and finding out about the current trending prices for that particular geographical area. Remember what I said earlier. You can actually find that within a mile or so, prices change considerably because of the perceived value of properties within a set area. If the house is located in a very popular area for single people, its value would be less to a family. Areas have reputations and these too will determine cost:

- Uptown trendy areas will be expensive and demand high prices

- Family friendly areas will be divided into upmarket and middle of the road.

- First time properties should be priced according to where they are

Ask yourself all kinds of questions. Is the property in an area where people can commute easily to the city? If so, that probably makes the property more valuable than in an area where commuting is difficult. Find out. Make it your business to check with local real estate agents and realtors to find out what that area is like. When the Property Brothers on TV buy a house, they know their locations. They know the market value of houses in a particular area and are able to buy properties with sufficient room to have money left over for renovations and still have a little extra value.

Say, for example, that you buy a home for $200,000 and it will cost you $100,000 to make it into a dream home for someone; will they be prepared to spend $300,000 or more within that given area? Know the answers; don't just guess them, as guessing isn't any good when you are talking about large investments.

You have to consider the location of the property and the various other factors such as age and depreciation value. You also need to know how active the market is and whether that market is gaining a lot of attention from potential buyers and renters.

You must also understand that you cannot land a cheap property and decide to renovate it and turn it into a multi-million property. It's a slow process. What you can do is work out your renovation costs, add this to the cost of the home and ask real estate agents if a house in new condition, which is refurbished would sell at the property price plus the renovations and a little profit. If the answer is no, you are in the wrong area.

If you don't check all this, then chances are you will not be able to make up for the expenses and end up undergoing loses. You must carefully consider how much you are paying and if it is worth it to you. Don't worry about walking away and don't be so keen to start your business that you are willing to take too many risks. It's not worth it.

How the Real Estate Market Works

We have cited that real estate markets can be unpredictable. We have also noted some of the strategies that you can apply to shield yourself against negative market forces. It is now time to look at a pictorial representation of how the real estate market dynamics interrelate to push prices up or down. The flow chart below captures the basic ways in which buyers and sellers interact with each other on the property market. You can also see the effect of particular changes on the market too.

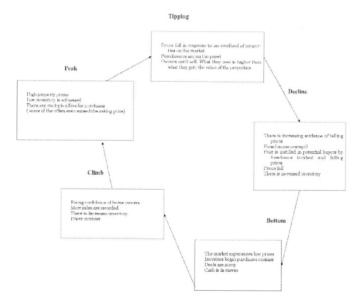

Summary

It is clear from the chart that there is more to buy than is obvious. The secret behind success in real estate markets is taking your time to study the markets. Analyze trends and act accordingly. It can all be summed up in the following

- Evaluate deals

- Buy the good ones

- Find good tenants/buyers

- Manage your property well

- Succeed

- Use funds derived from investment for more investment

Strategy 8: Value Consideration

When it comes to buying properties, especially for personal use, you have to consider the value of a house.

You might love a house and it might be the house that you see in your dreams. But it might not be in a preferred locality or might be too highly priced. You need to remove the element of personal likes and dislikes from the picture when you are buying houses to flip. It doesn't matter that you love it. It's not going to you who lives in it. You need to step back from feeling any emotional attachment to a house as when you feel that attachment, you tend to make mistakes. Just because you love the configuration of the house, doesn't mean someone else will.

It might also need a lot of renovation, which might cost you more than the house itself.

So before you jump into investing into a property, you have to assess the true value of a house. You have to ask yourself, "Will buyers love this place?" "Will buyers be happy here?" "Will a family be happy here?" These are just some of the questions that you must consider and if the answer to any of them is "No" then you must drop the plan.

You have to do a personal inspection and understand the house's various aspects. You must also judge whether the house is priced right and if it matches up to its real worth. That means assessing a lot of different aspects.

Strategy 9: Age/ Condition

Your fourth consideration must be assessing its age and condition. As a building or house ages, its upkeep becomes cumbersome and expensive.

Even if it is a multi-million dollar property, it will still require a fair share of renovation, which can further set you back a lot of money.

Quite often, buyers want the property at a lesser value, which might cause you to lose out on making up for the money that you spent on renovating it. That's why research is necessary before spending.

They might not agree with the type of renovations that you make and wish to not pay enough for it. In such cases, you can wait and not do up a place, until you score a potential buyer. It's actually a better practice to know your market first and to present potential buyers with a home which is neutral and spacious in appearance, which has a new kitchen and bathroom and which has neutral decoration throughout so that they can imagine their lives within that house. For this to work, you need to be in touch with your local tradesmen and know what different aspects of the renovation process will cost you. You also need to know that you can strike a deal with local suppliers of kitchen units, white goods and bathroom suites. Be up to date with the fittings, and don't skimp but if you let the suppliers know that you are going to be in the property business for a while and want decent discounts or you will go elsewhere, they are much more likely to package an attractive deal for you. Don't pay top dollar. Look at alternative packages and don't buy the cheapest either because people these days are not impressed with cheap presentation.

Even if they pay a little less for the property, as compared to your expectation, you will still be able to make a profit and not have to bear the renovating costs, but that takes knowing your market and catering for it correctly, using great discounts from your suppliers to help keep costs down. The only way that you are going to make money is to have a budget and keep within that budget, although it's wise to have a contingency fund to fall back on in the event of unexpected costs. For example, you may find that there is asbestos present on the property and this has to be removed by professionals and that costs money. You may find that the wall insulation has mold and you may have to replace it. You may also find that windows and doors are no longer up to code and have to replace these. Don't look for a cheap way out, as the potential buyer's inspector will notice things. Present your houses in a way that leaves no room for much negotiation and set your price at a level that meets the market head on but that also allows you to make a profit.

For example, you may be able to renovate existing kitchen cupboards but need new cooker, new worktops and to install an island. You can replace the doors on cabinets as long as the cupboards can be cleaned out like new. No one wants to buy a house with a dirty kitchen or dated bathroom so include these in your budget. The kinds of things that will add up in your price are these:

- Replacement flooring

- Tiling for bathroom and kitchen

- Worktop replacement

- Electrical changes to bring lighting up to modern standards

- Bathtubs and toilets

No one wants a second hand toilet. Recuperate what you can from a house and resell it to a salvage company rather than throwing it away. This helps you keep on track. If you are replacing tiles, try to find a tiling company that will do a deal on the prices because this can save you money. For flooring, lift carpets and look beneath them as often-older floors can be completely solid and in super condition which can save you money.

Strategy 10: Prior Problems

It is not just pure economical or monetary factors that influence the value of a property. In many instances, properties that would have witnessed a crime or a house that is set in a neighborhood where crimes are rife is likely to be available at a cheap price. This is due to the depreciation in value as perceived by the common public.

What you can do in such a case is invest in the property and hold on to it, until the locality improves and the danger of the house's past being questioned has passed.

The public tends to have a short memory and just within a couple of years' time, you can successfully sell the property with a decent profit margin. Only do this if you can afford to because there are dangers too. If you buy a home in a run-down area, are local people likely to break into the home? Is damage likely to be caused to the property during your ownership? It's only worthwhile buying in a run-down area if you know that work is being done to bring that particular area into a more upmarket condition.

If the property is located in a ghetto, forget it because people are unlikely to want to move into an area where there is already a reputation that puts their investment at risk. Neither should you because it's your living and you may find that houses like this won't sell no matter how cheap you make them appear to be. The problem associated with areas such as this are too great and it's far better to put your money into a more solid investment where you know that a market exists for houses at good prices. You need to be sure that you set standards and only buy within areas where these standards are met. These include:

- Is the market active?

- Does the house suit the kind of market you have in mind?

- Can you make money on the house even after your renovation costs?

- Is the property worth keeping hold of as a rental until prices increase?

- Can you afford the price of the house plus the renovations?

The house that you buy has to attract a certain kind of buyer. If you cannot envisage the market because the house is badly situated or borderline interesting to a particular set of people, walk away. You can't afford the risk. If it is what you can instantly see as an investment that will pay off, then that's a different story.

CHAPTER 5

THE 5 DEAL MAKERS

Now that we have looked at the 5 main criteria for you to consider in terms of a property's true worth, let us now look at the 5 types of deals that you can strike, when you invest in a property. This gives you an idea of the kind of sales that exist and how to take advantage of them. Not all sales are the same, so you need this information to guide you toward a market that will help you to maximize your potential.

Strategy 11: Auction wisely

Auctioning is one of the best ways for you to land good deals and can also be one of the worst ways. It is great because you are in command and you can decide how much you want to spend but it can be bad, if you get carried away and end up paying more than the property's true value. We warned you about this in a previous chapter, but you really do need to inspect the property, decide upon what it will cost to renovate and then work out if there is a margin for profit to be made on the house.

So the best thing for you to do is to find out the true value of the property and go in with a budget that is 10% more than the initial asking price at auction. That should be your last limit and if someone else is bidding higher, then you should simply let go. And if you feel that the property is worth it, then you can make just a 5% higher bid for it but be prepared to cut down a little on your renovation costs to make sure your profit margin is intact. If you are aware of the other bidder's strategies, then you can decide accordingly. Personally, I find auctions are a little difficult. You have to have your finance in place or have the cash. If you don't, don't even bother with them. You need to talk to your bank and agree in advance what they are prepared to lend you because you need finances to be straightforward and auction houses ask that people pay straight away. That means you are the owner from the moment the money switches hands. You need to be ready to turn-over that house, to get in and do the repairs and sometimes because of the doubt element when bidding against others, you can't have your workforce ready to do that.

If you have a regular set up where you can move workers from one job to another, however, auction houses offer a great opportunity. You can have unskilled workers go in the clear the house ready for first and second fit. That may mean pulling down existing tiling, getting rid of kitchens, getting rid of baths, etc. but do remember where plumbing is concerned that you need to have a plumber disconnect items ready for removal.

Strategy 12: Look for Distress sales

Distress sales are one of the best ways for you to score a great deal. When it comes to such sales, the owner will be in a hurry to get rid or dispose of a property owing to having to move countries and other such reasons. In such a case, the priority of the owner or seller will either be quick disposal of property or realization of consideration. They will not have the time or the inclination to haggle over the prices to make some profit. This mentality of the seller should be capitalized on and your reaction should be to play hardball. This may be in the case of someone selling up to pay off an ex and thus say goodbye to a period of their lives, which is regrettable. It may also be because someone has died and the property is just money tied up with no sentimental value. Whatever the reason, the one thing that you can be sure of is that the owner is no longer attached to the property and sees it as a noose around his/her neck. These people want to get rid of the house and quickly.

Always be on a look out for such sales, as you can score the property for less and make a huge profit on it. Even if you don't dispose of it, you will get the opportunity to rent it out, and can splurge on doing up the interiors to suit that market. The way to look for these is to try and talk to the seller and get a feel for the place. A couple of good indications are that the house looks un-loved and uncared for and may be not lived in any more although there are still some reminders of the life that was lived in it. Usually when people sell houses in this way, they don't actually live there anymore and the house is surplus to requirements. Thus the garden may look untended even if the house is in a pretty good area.

At the same time, buying and holding such a house can be more advantageous as compared with flipping it. The property might rise in value, thereby helping you score better and higher profits. Keep your eyes peeled as most distress sales get sold at lightning speed and if you are late then you will miss out on a great opportunity. Ask your real estate agents to let you know and let them know that you have cash ready because it's more interesting for them to tell you if they know they are likely to achieve a sale. Look out for private ads as well because perhaps the house will be sold privately because of frustration and cost of hiring a real estate agent.

Strategy 13: Be present at Foreclosures

Foreclosures are one of the best ways for you to buy a great property, at a discounted price.

When it comes to foreclosures, the creditor only plans to make back whatever was lent and not a penny more. So you will end up landing a property at a highly discounted price and can immediately flip it, to make a big profit. The house may be in good condition or may simply need tidying up a little and staging for sale. Often these houses look a little untidy or shabby because the owners don't have the money for expensive upkeep. Before you even consider flipping the house, make sure it's presentable. Often a quick coat of neutral paint and hired furniture can make the place look a lot more valuable than it did when you bought it and the cost of hired furniture for open day really isn't that expensive. Other things that will help will be to strip the house of old carpets. Often you find that there are perfectly good floors beneath them and carpets are really not the vogue at the moment so it will make the interior look a lot more up to date and ready for someone to move into.

Now let's look at an example to understand it better. Let's say "A" bought a house where he paid 20% from his pocket and the rest was a loan. Now if he ended up paying say 20% of the 80% that he borrowed and is unable to pay the rest, then the creditor will foreclose the house and try to make up for that unpaid amount alone.

So you can score a good property at a very low price, and sell it at a high price. Most foreclosures are not made public and you might want to do regular scouring's in your area to be aware of one. Where do you find foreclosures? The Department of Housing and Urban Development has details of all homes where the owners have been served with foreclosure notices. This means that you can keep up to date with information on their website. This is a completely free of charge resource that is a must for anyone who feels that they want to get in on the act of buying homes which are up for foreclosure.

Strategy 14: Understanding Outright Sale

Buying a house outright is one of the best ways of buying a property. There are no special arrangements and the deal is clear and easy. That is why cash purchasers will always get the preference by owners. They want no hassle and if a house is sold subject to a loan, there is always going to be a waiting time until banks release funds.

When there is a house for sale, you will be required to purchase it by paying the full amount. If you are unable to raise enough money, then you can avail a loan. If you are going to take out a loan, have this arranged in advance and it's almost as good as a cash sale as long as you have written confirmation from your bank of the amount they are prepared to advance you. And in order to repay that loan, you can rent the place out if you want to. However, do research on whether the area has a glut of rental properties or whether there is a need and what kind of people will rent property in that particular area.

If you aim for business people and the area is more for families or students, then you may be doing refurbishment work that won't give you the returns that you expect. It's your job, as a professional to check out what the market is like for rentals and what kind of income this is likely to give you because this will also show you whether the rental that you can expect will actually cover the amount of the loan that you take out. Get the bank to draw up paperwork to give you a clear demonstration of the term of the loan, and also what the monthly repayments would be. Find out what tenants pay in the way of housing taxes and what you as an owner will be expected to pay. You need all the information that you can get so that you don't make mistaken purchases and end up with a property that you cannot shift.

But you have to be careful while buying a property outright, as there might be a million things that you may have to consider first. For example, don't be quick to part with cash until you are happy that an expert's report says that the house is in good sound condition. It may cost money for the report, but your offer should always be subject to satisfactory reports. That way, you cover yourself in case these reports find asbestos, which is expensive to remove; mold and damp which may need extra cash injection to fix or has any subsidence problem. Be aware of all of these considerations when you are buying in an area, which is prone to storms and bad weather.

You must scour all possible online sites to look for what property is available and once you find the best deal, you must not waste time and invest in it as soon as you can within the limits of sensibility. You can offer subject to reports and that will safeguard you in the event of costly repairs having to be done.

Strategy 15: Buy-Move-Sell

When you buy a property, you can move in and then dispose of it after a couple of years. Many reasons such as recession and other such problems might cause people to not be interested in buying a house. What you do need to know is what the law is with regard to buying a house and selling it once it's refurbished. There may even be a law that states that you need to pay capital gains tax if you buy over a certain number of properties in your state, so do check this.

This will apply to a certain number of houses, although if you are registered as a housing development company, you may find that the figure changes as applied to a company, rather than to an individual. If you are disinterested in renting it out, owing to the problems that tenants bring along, then you can simply move into the house yourself. And when you feel that the property's value has increased, you can sell it and make a profit. You can also have a relative live in, just to keep the house occupied and prevent excess dust and dirt accumulating. The only problem with the last two solutions is that neither pays the amount you borrowed on the house, whereas a tenancy could. If you buy, move, sell, the property would be your own main residence and may not be counted from a capital gains point of view, but do talk to an accountant in advance to establish if this is the case.

CHAPTER 6

OWNERSHIP AND ACQUISITION RIGHTS

Many times, you will want to invest in a property but you will not have the resources for it. In such cases, here are a few options for you to try out to enable you to be able to invest in the properties of your dreams.

Strategy 16: Joint Acquisition with Family Members

In a joint acquisition, you can team up with a family member to help you land a property. This will also involve sharing profits and perhaps you have family members that want to try this business with you.

You can ask them to invest simultaneously and acquire a property. You will have to work out and iron out all the details before jumping into it. It's best to do this through a lawyer so that an agreement is written up that covers your interests as well as theirs.

And when in such a joint holding, both of you will have a share in the property and you have to take joint decisions on the property. Don't do this with a family member you know to be unrealistic as it can cause rifts in your relationship. However, you may find that a relative is prepared to put in cash but may not want to be involved in the renovation and is perfectly happy that you simply repay the debt when you sell the house.

But if you have your relative "gift" the property to you, then you can enjoy the full benefits of it. However, be aware that the law doesn't always approve of this kind of transaction because it is almost like getting a capital gain through a relative. Check all details with an accountant before you take this route.

Strategy 17: Joint Acquisition with a Stranger

Often, you will find like-minded people in the various parties and meetings that you attend.

And if you find a reliable agent who is interested in the same property as you, then you can invest in a property together but make it official so that your financial interests are protected. The problem with this kind of deal is that you may find yourself disagreeing about the kind of renovations that need to be done to earn money on the property so you really need to know that your new partner is thinking on the same lines as you.

You must decide on who pays which bills and if you are going to be owners with the same rights. For example, is this a silent partner who is merely funding based on the potential profit you can make from a house? If so, there will be limitations since his lawyer is likely to put a time limit on the loan used from that person and you need to comply with it and finish the work on time to repay him. If he is going to be a working partner, you need everything written down so there are no disagreements that put the investment at jeopardy.

At the same time, you must be careful in identifying the various people and understand their intentions thoroughly. You must not jump into deals without doing a background check of these realtors/ agents.

You can start by investing in a small property first and then move to a bigger one. Do not start investing in big projects first. You must do it step by step.

And it does not always have to be a stranger; you can ask a friend or an acquaintance, who is keen on making an investment. Again, it's essential to have all the legal aspects ironed out so that you know exactly what the terms of his investment are and what they mean to the timescale in which you have to renovate and sell the property in question.

I mention this because some people are sick of investing in banks these days and see investment in property as being much more of a sure thing. Thus, they are prepared to help out provided that they make something on their money that is more than the bank would have paid them. Thus, if you are thinking of doing this kind of business, you need to make sure that there's enough equity in the house for both partners to gain, rather than do all the work and then find the terms of the contract mean that the majority will go to the partner who did nothing other than supplying the funds.

Strategy 18: Using inherited Properties for profit

When you inherit a property, you have to be smart about it. You have to decide on whether you wish to hold on to it or sell it and if you do, will you be able to make a huge profit out of it.

If it is only going to garner a small profit, then it is better to hold on to it. You might also want to do it up before you attempt to sell it as it is likely to be a little outdated and this will help to achieve a good price for the house. If it is of sentimental value and you don't want to dispose of it, you could use it as a potential rental property but it will still need to be refurbished and repairs done before you undertake this. Otherwise, you are likely to have unforeseen costs in the future and you certainly need to avoid this.

Discuss the inheritance with your lawyer to find out what the financial implications are as there may be debts that are also inherited. Find out the full story and discuss with your lawyer the implications of inheritance so that your legal options are explained to you.

You can also decide whether you would like to move in or rent it out.

If you already have your own place, then decide on which house will help you get a better rent. Depending on the choice you make, you can let the other house out for rent and potentially move into the inheritance property, if you feel that this is a good move for your family.

You may find that holding onto inheritance properties is the best bet because it could get higher in value. It's really down to where the property is and what the market is like at the time that you inherit. You need to check into all of this before you make a decision.

Strategy 19: Rightful Share

Many times, you might have a rightful share to a property and might be oblivious to it. You can consider talking to your parents and finding out as to the properties that you will inherit. Being proactive will help and you will be able to decide on a future course of action. If you are an heir to a property, and if someone or something is preventing you from getting your rightful share, then you can, by all means, have the law intervene and help you out.

Before you do, you can do a small research of what is really happening and who is controlling the property. If you live in another state or country, then it would be advisable for you to move to the city or country where the property is located.

Once you claim your rightful share, you can decide as to what you would like to do with it in conjunction with anyone else who has a share. In general discussion with family, you may find that aunts, uncles or someone else in the family intends to leave you a property and may even include that the property be divided between you and your siblings. In a case such as this, you will need to make sure that everyone agrees on the course of action that is taken. For example, one sibling may want to keep the property while others want to sell and can buy them out by giving them their share in cash.

Strategy 20: Funded Acquisition

A funded acquisition is one where a company will help you acquire that property. They will invest in it or assist you in investing.

In order for you to land such a deal, you must be at the top of your game and approachable by big companies.

Once the property is acquired, you can rent it out or sell it to a big brand company and share the profits with the company that invested along with you. Even if you are just the dealmaker between the company and the property owners, then you can make a profit out of it. Find out what large companies exist in your area and it may even be worthwhile dropping in to discuss such a plan, but do expect them to want to see other jobs that you have completed.

CHAPTER 7

THE DON'TS OF REAL ESTATE

Up until now, we have looked at the various strategies you need to adopt in order to land a good property deal. In this chapter, I shed some light on the various things that you must not do while you are investing in real estate.

Strategy 21: Don't Be Over Confident

One of the main rules while investing in real estate is that you cannot be too confident. If you think that you will be the most successful person in real estate, then that would be an assumption based on guesswork. Wait until you know what you are doing and have earned that confidence for being able to turn over homes quickly and efficiently. Even then, surprises can happen and it's never worth being overly confident.

The industry welcomes everybody with open arms no doubt, but it will also not be as easy as you first think – at least until you have gained the experience needed. The Property Brothers TV show is a good example of professionalism. They know their business, and they are very good at turning fixer uppers into great homes, which are up to date and fit the dreams of the people who buy them. However, even they make mistakes sometimes, which is because of hidden defects. You never know what you may find when you start to refurbish a home. Thus, always have a contingency, or put aside sufficient money to meet extra costs if and when they occur. In other words, cover the worst-case scenario.

You will have to put in a lot of hard work and only then will you be able to make profits. But no matter what the case, you must never give up. There will be a lot of downs initially, but once you get the hang of it, you will start to enjoy what you are doing and will have more experience of working with contractors and knowing which ones are reliable and reasonable in cost.

And it does not have to be your main business. You can flip houses part time as a business and help add to your existing income. The only snag with this is that it pays to keep an eye on the order the work is being done in and making sure that contractors keep up with their schedules. It's harder to do this if you are working full time unless your work allows you the freedom to actually go in and make your presence felt regularly.

And to become the best, you must learn from the best. Take up an internship at a top firm, just to understand the various ways in which the real estate industry operates.

You can then venture out on your own and slowly but steadily, make progress. If you don't want to work for someone else, then at least know that the contractors you hire are reliable. Don't take the first quotations you get. Try several and ask them lots of questions. Someone who is adaptable and who is willing to work with you also needs to be someone who understands you and who you get on with well, so that they are motivated to get the work done on time. The problem is that if you have contractors waiting to get on with their jobs because others have not done the preparation that wastes both time and money.

Strategy 22: Don't Expect Quick Results

The world of real estate is one, where quick results are never found. It takes a little time for you to settle in and see results.

Overnight success is an impossible scenario, as nobody can strike gold within the first few attempts. Patience should be your virtue, if you wish to make it big in the world of real estate. With manageable projects, you can more easily buy, renovate, and sell the home and you can even make more profit by taking on many of the renovation jobs yourself. Avoid doing plumbing and electrical work unless you are qualified to do it. The areas where you can save money and jobs, which are reasonably simple for you to do are:

- Painting and decorating

- Tiling and flooring

- All the preparation work as this is really a matter of labor rather than skill

You will have to invest and wait for some time, in order for the value of the property to grow. This is the time that it takes to renovate a property and prepare it for the market but you should also have your eye on the next investment, so that there is no wasted time between houses, especially if you want to have a constant flow of cash coming in and use that which you need to spend on renovations without having to borrow more money. Eventually, you will find that as your profit margins increase, you may be investing cash instead of borrowing, but that doesn't make the timescale less critical. Every moment that you own the property, you have extra costs to pay, so the sooner you get your house flipped, the better from a financial standpoint.

It might take you at least 2 to 3 years to establish yourself as a successful real estate investor, but it doesn't have to. Some people through researching the market correctly have been able to impress real estate agents with the quality of the renovations that have been done and if a real estate agent believes in what you have for sale, it will sell more quickly.

You will have to do extensive research and understand the market trends. You have to understand as to where and how you can invest and make all the right choices. Even if you make a wrong choice, you have to learn to rectify it or recover financially from it. You cannot let one or two bad experiences put you off. It's really a question of following the same procedure every time.

- Know your house values for the geographical area

- Compare like to like

- Work out if you can purchase the house and renovate it and still sell at a profit.

Only through consistent hard work and patience, will you be able to make it big in the world of real estate investing. There is a lot of money to be made in real estate but you need a very realistic approach. Don't just dream it. Plan it and have everything worked out on paper such as:

- A timetable for repairs

- Contractors ready to get working within set time scales

- A reliable real estate agent to sell the home

Investment in real estate is not an overnight stunt. Many real estate busy bodies peddle the lie around. Do not buy it. There are no rugs to riches overnight in real estate. In fact, it is one of those investments that require a significant initial input. Such an input takes time to assemble. Do not believe the ads on billboards and TV or websites either. They are always driven by a yearning to make some extra money. This inclination effectively clouds objectivity.

Strategy 23: Don't Miscalculate

It is foolish to use the figures you get from research exactly as they are. There are many unknown aspects of the investment that you are not privy to before you make a payment. You also need to double the time estimates for returns as a realistic stress free guarantee.

Never miscalculate when it comes to investing. If you are into investing in big time properties such as buildings, then you must be very particular about the math that will be involved. I missed an opportunity once because I looked at the asking price and thought it was beyond my scope. The unfortunate thing was that the guy who bought this particular block of apartments made an absolute fortune. He had worked out the potential and I hadn't looked further than the asking price. Bought and paid for, cleaned up and sold off in individual units, he managed to double his money and that's some investment! The problem was that I hadn't done the math, and had merely been afraid of the asking price thinking that it was beyond my scope. In fact, the bank told me in a meeting that they would have been glad to lend me the funds short term at a special rate had I had the faith in myself to invest in such an opportunity.

Misjudging the cash flow

If you don't factor the dark possibilities in your plan for a real estate purchase, it could easily become a liability. There are times when properties stay for extended periods before they are occupied by tenants. Meanwhile, your lenders do not consider the reality that you are not earning from your investment. Remember, formal loan facilities will require servicing consistently. You are also likely to be incurring other costs such as maintenance insurance and local authority taxes. If you didn't plan for these eventualities, you will be seriously stressed.

You must maintain a journal or have software installed, that will allow you to keep tab of all your investments. You have to understand the ways in which you must maintain a balance between your available cash flow and outflow. Keeping everything on budget is essential. When you fix a budget for repairs, make sure that you don't get carried away in the shops by buying more expensive fittings just because they look nice. Decide on the fittings based on quality for price and stick with your original plans. To do otherwise will cut into your contingency meaning that you will make less profit.

And if you are finding it difficult then you can hire an assistant or an accountant to help you out. If you find it too expensive to hire one, then you can enlist the help of a friend who perhaps has a good head for project management.

If you do miscalculate, then immediately let the other party know about it. You can also buy some time and correct all your mistakes. But never go ahead with a deal knowing that you have miscalculations, which can cause you to undergo a loss. By covering yourself when you make an offer on a home, by inserting a clause that the offer is made subject to satisfactory expert reports, you don't make that kind of error. If you buy without looking into this side of things, you are likely to make mistakes.

Strategy 24: Don't Over Pay Taxes

Investing in real estate is seen as being one of the best ways to cut down on paying taxes. Several people invest in real estate just so that a certain amount of tax can be saved.

When you raise a loan to buy a property, you can save the same amount of tax. And once you have paid the tax, you can repay the loan.

You can buy a property just before filing for tax and then sell it off within a couple of months. You can do this on a yearly basis. To get full information on any tax incentives, do ask an accountant. It will be worth paying for the appointment just to have that knowledge.

At the same time, when it comes to real estate investing, you have to carefully consider the various taxes that you will be required to pay. An accountant can help you with this. The other thing to consider is that there may be grants available to improve the home within the area where you are buying. If this is the case, make sure that you comply with all the regulations. In this way, you may receive help for double-glazing, for updating the heating system or for anything, which helps the home to conserve energy

There can be ways in which you can cut down on the taxes that you pay. You must read up on it and do your research on the same.

Certain elements, which are considered by the government as improvements to energy levels may give tax incentives. I can't be more specific as these are different in all areas but as someone who wants to make money from flipping or renting homes, you need to be aware of your rights and privileges and this will help you considerably when choosing a home to purchase.

You can also hire a chartered accountant to help you out. Ultimately, you must be able to save on the taxes that you pay and pay the least possible while acquiring a property.

Strategy 25: Have Strong Connections

When it comes to real estate, you have to have strong connections. You have to have the right set of friends, who will count you in and let you know of a good opportunity. You also need to have a good set of workers who are available when you need them and are reliable enough for you to depend upon.

You have to join communities and attend agent meetings. You must take part in property fairs and get yourself noticed. This is important because there may be homes that come up for sale and that need someone to purchase them quickly. Thus, if real estate agents know that you are likely to be interested, they will keep you informed of properties, which match that criteria and which are on the market at prices, which will give you a good profit margin.

Remember that only you can promote yourself and no one else. Unless you get recognized as a bona fide realtor, people will hesitate to approach you and you will miss out on some good opportunities. Investing in flyers to give out to people at any property meetings or to pass to real estate agents in your area to let them know of the services that you provide may just help them to make a sale and you to make a killing on the price of a house.

So remember to advertise yourself as widely and as well as possible. Have a set of calling cards printed. These are very cheap now on the Internet and having them with you at all times will help you to be able to leave them should a potential lead to a good property ask for your details. If you don't have a calling card, the person who does is much more likely to get the call from an agent when a property that's interesting comes up. Make your cards good quality and always answer all of your emails on time. Otherwise, you may just kick yourself for missing out on a wonderful opportunity.

Other Terrible Mistakes in Real Estate Investment

Planning as you go

One of the common mistakes new real estate investors make is to treat real estate investment as though it is a transaction. You should never venture in real estate, commit yourself, time, and money and then proceed to plan afterwards. Never buy then start planning. This is like attempting to get to a destination before you learn the best routes or just even the route. You may as well find yourself in the exact opposite direction. Real estate investment is a business and not just a transaction. This means it is something that is going to consume your time and resources over a period. One of the startling things I've always advised my friends and students who pursue real estate investment is that it is never a good idea to embrace properties for emotional purposes. You should only use numbers to guide you when it comes to real estate investment or any other investment for that matter. Make several offers for properties and pick one that best suits you. Your choice should of course be guided by the possible returns you realistically project compared to the input.

Do not rely on looks to make decisions on real estate investment. Once you succeed to cut out emotion by focusing on figures, you are better placed to make sensible offers based on what you will gain from the purchase or sell.

The Lone Ranger Syndrome

Although investment is a personal matter, it is one that reins in many persons. There is no such thing as secrecy in real estate investment. You need to build an investment team in real estate business. Such a team should constitute people who bring different skills to the table of business. Some of the people you need to call to your team include:

- A property valuer or appraiser

- A home inspector

- A lender

- A closing attorney

- A maintenance team such as plumbers, electricians, painters, air conditioner experts, landscapers, flooring experts, and even cleaners

- A house equipment supplier such as a hardware dealer

This team will be important as you buy and sell or rent out property. They will also save you a lot of time and inconvenience that often arises in managing your properties.

Overpaying

One thing that should always be at your fingertips is that any excess money you put in real estate investment renders the property less profitable. It is easy to overpay in real estate. Usually, the sellers offer their price 25% to even 50% over the real value of the targeted property. The dealers will try to convince you against all odds that their price is the fairest. Be prudent and conduct independent searches for pricing. The Real estate trends cycle chart on planning in this book will help you come to grips with dynamics that dictate prices and events around real estate investments.

Poor back grounding

This is a term I coined from the need to do a background check on all property you wish to purchase. Read all the available materials relating to your target niche. You need to take a walk both on site and on the Internet. Search for information relating to the properties you are targeting. Look out for any reviews of the dealers/sellers. Find out the potentials and the downsides of investing in your targeted property.

Back grounding also involves searches through the relevant authorities on licenses and encumbrances that may be linked to the property. Have all the facts right before you engage. Even then, keep all your cards close to your chest. Keep asking questions about the property you want to purchase. If you conduct sufficient research on the property in question before you engage in negotiations with the dealers, you are likely to have a lot to ask about.

As you listen to the responses from the dealers, you need to learn to listen well. Do not concentrate on what you want to get from the deal. You also need to listen to what is not being said. What is not being said is often more important in any business.

Rush Through

Many new investors tend to rush to acquire property. This is often caused by panic. People strive to save for investment for many years. When their check finally comes through, they find themselves in a situation. They are too scared to keep their money in their accounts for fear of misusing it. Since it is a preplanned business move they have always carried on their mind, they will tend to fall for the first good-looking deal they come across. This can be costly business-wise. Dealers know when they are handling a newbie. They will peak their bargain to reap from the rare opportunity. Do not be a statistic on the list of those who plundered their hard-earned savings. Take your time to sample the options at your disposal. Some of the measures you need to take include

- Viewing the property several times

- Getting an inspector to inspect the property before you start making strong commitments

- Finding out the true cost of repairs of a house or whatever premise you want to purchase. You will use such information to ask for price reduction.

Reducing volumes

You should try to run several deals simultaneously. This way, you are likely to balance out the low points with the high points. Any successful real estate investment requires running high volumes.

Pushing yourself to a corner

Before you purchase a piece of property, you need to figure out the possible options for your investment. Think of a scenario where it becomes hard to rent out or lease. You need to figure out exit possibilities. You need to develop such a plan that will cover you. Come up with not only plan A, but also plans B, C and D.

Plan A for your investment could be a makeover, B. could be to hold and sell, C. could be a lease, and D could be selling immediately. Having a contingency for your business plans helps you stay free and confident. You will, therefore be at ease even when the markets for a particular niche plunges suddenly.

CHAPTER 8

TOP REAL ESTATE
STRATEGIES

If you are a real estate company, an individual in the business or a seller trying to sell your property, this chapter has insights for everyone concerned. This is an update of what has been written in the previous chapters. These strategies will sum up as core strategies to enhance your knowledge and power to deal with the most critical situations in real estate.

A Discussion Leading to a Solution

Out of all the strategies explained, the first and foremost still remains as the basic questions asked in a simple way. You need to ask yourself these questions repeatedly and conclude in way that everyone understands and adheres to. These questions are much needed for self-introspection and if you are an organization working towards your real estate strategies.

When you want to understand what your goal is, what your end point is and why you want to take up this task, it is better to know the answers before you jump into these situations. If you are an organization then understand what your core strategies are, why you want to get into this area of business and what kind of returns you can expect from your investment. For example, do you want to cash in on an area, which is being improved? Do you want to provide reasonable property for people to rent? Are you versed in all of the different areas of renovation and have a good idea of what repairs cost?

A new leadership agenda is taking shape where leaders are asking the right questions before taking action versus taking action and then asking exploratory questions. Understanding "why" and "what" will enable the entire organization to enter 2014 into a new venture and beyond with confidence, balance and engaged talent.

And if you are an individual dealing in real estate business then you are the master of your destiny. You should then take careful steps have an agenda that suits you and create avenues for profits, by knowing what you can afford to spend, what repairs will cost and what profit margin you have.

Focus is the Key

There are far too many distractions, disruptions, and disruptions in the daily events of a real estate firm and the industry per se. New deals, once-in-a-lifetime prospects, new business endeavors and surprises appear to be the norm. However, these actions redirect time, resources and energy away from core business activities of an individual or an organization dealing in real estate business.

When a real estate organization becomes less proactive and day-to-day, it loses its competitive edge, overall efficiency declines, profitability is reduced and frustration creeps into leadership interactions. The same applies to an individual who lacks focus. Everyone has 24 hours in a day to accomplish great things; therefore, it is not a lack of time but a lack of focus that separates the winners from the losers.

After decades of scrutinizing human nature within real estate firms, I am firmly convinced that all real estate organizations and individuals to a larger extent are destined to become unfocused. Whether by diversification, extension of current business or failure to acknowledge and respond to customer life cycles, staying focused continues as a major challenge for many.

More money can be made in specialist areas than in generalities. More money can be made when one is a perceived professional versus a commodity option. The power of contracting, not expanding, the base will result in a significant likelihood for increasing market and customer share.

One of the great techniques for staying focused is to prepare Action Plans with specific time lines. Identifying the top five "must-do" actions to be completed within a stipulated period keeps an organization focused and the leadership aligned.

It doesn't matter if you are a one-man army trying to accomplish your goals; this pattern still works for you. You could have it written on your wall for that focus to come in all the time. Getting and remaining focused for the planned year will set the ball rolling.

One guy I knew aimed at providing warden accommodation for elderly people. He had contractors who fitted individual houses with alarms so that elderly people could feel safe within their own homes. He also knew exactly what adaptations needed to be made so that the premises were always user-friendly for those with limited movement or who were aged. He stayed within that market and by doing that could specialize in exactly the right trades that he needed getting regular discounted prices and being able to provide secure premises for elderly people who were downsizing.

Wake Up and Walk Again – Focus & Value

Success in the real estate industry is not a matter of intensity, but of balance, synergy and compatibility among clients, assets, markets, capital and resources. There is a finite limit to the scaling of investments and operations where knowledge, insights, oversight and relationships cannot be sustained at the highest level.

Everyone in the business must take a critical look at shedding those assets, business units, services and client relationships that are described using the words "it's tough out there", very expensive to maintain, too little profit, too distracting and too disruptive to all of them in the business.

Yes, I know that may mean selling legacy assets or businesses, discontinuing business lines that have-been-with-us-forever and winding down activities that involve a number of dedicated professionals and narrowing down your business areas. If the primary purpose of real estate firms or individuals is to make money, then rebalancing one's asset and operational platform is critical.

Further, there are three key components regarding value: creating value, adding value and protecting value. Moving forward with the right platform and with the right people at the right time requires making the right choices, not the most suitable decisions. Strengthening the core begins with shedding the non-essential.

The contest, however, is not the "getting out," but determining what and how to replace that income. William Wordsworth, once said, "Let us learn from the past to yield by the present and from the present to live better in the future." Over the next few years, tightrope walking will prevail, better to get it right now than have to painfully correct in the future.

Leaders and industry experts at all levels are focused on creating flexibility throughout an organization and the industry on the whole. In the coming years, focusing on value will be critical to exceeding all stakeholders' expectations.

What this means to you is to know the following:

- How long will you own a house?

- What is your projected project time?

- How will you ensure that you meet this?

- Building programs so that you are not holding onto assets, which should be giving you income.

Be Clear and Have a Vision

This key strategy has consistently made to the top list of must-have strategies since the beginning of the real estate industry. Without a clear vision, how does an organization or an individual know what they are trying to achieve or where they are going? And, if you don't know where you are going, all roads lead there.

In today's highly competitive marketplace, and in an age of rising expectations, having a clear vision is a must. A vision is more than a testimonial of what might happen, it is a call to action on what can happen. A good vision proclamation must be memorable, assessable, and motivating. It must be short and recommended by all company leaders if you are an organization.

In the coming years, real estate leaders need to let go of outcomes and focus on doing one's best in alignment with the organization's vision and long-range goals. Where there is clarity of vision, there must be clarity of purpose, clarity of action and clarity of priorities. Without a vision statement, all decisions can only be made in the "now" with little or no connectivity to tomorrow. Winging it isn't an option. Perhaps you want to provide homes that adhere to a certain standard. Perhaps you want to give people what it is that they are seeking. Your renovation of houses must meet the existing market. That's why it's so important to know what the given market is within the area where you are buying homes. Your vision for that home is only complete if you know the following:

- Approximate price and timescale of the renovation work

- Initial Cost

- Type of people who are looking for homes in your area

- What else is available to them

A vision is aspirational and inspirational. A vision statement is not a strategic plan, but merely articulates where you are going. A strategic plan describes how to get there.

Hardly a day goes by in a real estate firm without someone asking or thinking, "Where are we going, why are we doing this and what is the goal?" With the power of visioning, there is no confusion of direction, purpose, or priority. Because vision statements are future-based and meant to inspire an organization, they are for internal consumption. A mission statement states what you do and for whom, where you do it, and for the benefit of whom; a very external, feel-good statement.

If you are an independent real estate businessman, you should still have your goals set and a vision that will guide you. Your vision should include the full picture from purchase of a home right through the renovation process and eventual sale to the target market. If you don't know the market, which is active in the area where you are thinking of buying, ensure that you do more research before you invest because if you target the wrong market, you are likely to lose money.

Be Prepared

It is not the time to sit back, pause, react and respond. It is the time to prepare for a future of limitless possibilities. By following the previous strategies, you will be ready for a time full of surprises, challenges, disappointments, and incredible events. Being a real estate expert, you must incorporate risk scenarios into strategic planning.

- Know that your workforce is available from the date of purchase
- Know the timescales for each set of work.

You will have to use unskilled workers to carry out any preparation works, such as knocking down interior walls, taking out old fittings, kitchens and bathrooms, but you also need to know the delivery dates for all the items you need to buy. Remember, made to measure is always expensive. Fit your home with off the shelf units and make sure that your plans are measured twice to ensure that everything fits as it should without having expensive errors.

Having the confidence to grow, enter new markets, do different things and lead a collaborative environment is a must. And for organizations, driving innovation, while managing costs, will be important in years ahead. Being risk resistant, identifying opportunities before others, creating value and growing a valued customer base are equally of value.

I would encourage every real estate expert to ask the following questions every now and then, perhaps posting them on your walls as a reminder:

- What three interesting things did I do today?

- What did I do to get more customers?

- What did I do to get a step ahead of our competitors?

- What is the area that needs improvement for tomorrow?

- How can I perform better?

Moving from excellence to performance will cause you to always strive and to become better in all you do. It has been said that knowing something does nothing, but doing something makes a difference. If you have a bad day, don't let it get you down. You may discover something you didn't know you had to fix, but that's all part and parcel of the renovation game. That's why you have a contingency fund available. Sometimes you win and sometimes you lose, but that contingency is what stops you from going bankrupt. If an electrician says he will do the job for $20,000, count $22,000 and always overestimate everything to allow for little things that may happen during the course of the work. If you overestimate your costs, you are likely to keep on budget and may even have more money left at the end of the renovation than you thought, thus increasing your profit margin.

If you have workers that are good at working to set timings, you don't lose even more money. Having a regular crew of workers is well worth it once you get established, because they know that if they do a good job, there's more work waiting for them on future projects.

Don't be afraid to get rid of slackers. You can't afford to have workers who don't pull their weight. If you find mistakes being made on a regular basis, you may need to assess whether the staff you are using are being used for the right jobs. When pulling down internal walls, for example, bull at a gate isn't the way to handle it. There may be electrical wiring within walls and your workforce needs to be aware that bad work may cost you more money and that you're not prepared to continue to employ those who show lack of common sense.

CHAPTER 9

GOLDEN METHODS IN REAL ESTATE INVESTING

These principles will guide you to make the right decisions and will create a thought in your mind before you take any decision. The methods stated below are carefully researched and the top ones are chosen for your benefit.

Wraparound Method

Wraparound financing yields big savings for buyers at the same time that it puts profits into the pocket of the seller. Only the lender gets shortchanged.

An example:

Imagine you offer to buy the property for $200,000. If the seller agrees to finance $180,000 at 7.5 percent fully amortized over 20 years, your payment (P&I) equals $1,450 per month.

Points to consider:

- The underlying $100,000 mortgage remains in place, and its monthly payments will be paid by the seller.

- To complete the purchase, you sign a land contract, mortgage, or trust deed with the seller.

- Each month the seller collects $1,450 from you and pays the bank a monthly mortgage payment of $716 for a net in the seller's pocket of $734 ($1,450 less $716). Because the seller has actually financed only $80,000 ($180,000 less the 100,000 still owed to the bank), he achieves an attractive rate of return on his loan of 11.1 percent.

- In spite of this you still gain.

- Had you financed $180,000 with a bank at the market rate of 9 percent amortized over 20 years, your payment would total $1,619 per month instead of the $1,450 that you'll pay to the seller.

- The actual spread between the current market interest rate, the seller's old bank rate, and the interest rate you pay the seller will depend on the motives and negotiating power of you and the seller.

Please note that the above example shows how a wraparound can benefit both parties—true win-win financing.

Leasing Options

Are you looking to own a property?

Yet, for reasons of stained credit, self-employment (especially those with off-the-books income or tax minimized income), unstable income (commissions, tips), or lack of cash, do you believe that you can't currently qualify for a mortgage from a lending institution?

Then the lease option (a lease with an option to purchase) might solve your dilemma. Properly structured, the lease option will permit you to acquire ownership rights in a property. At the same time, it also gives you time to improve your financial profile.

MAKE IT WORK FOR YOU

As the name implies, the lease option combines two contracts into one: a lease and an option to buy. Under the lease, you sign a rental agreement that covers the usual rental terms and conditions such as:

- Monthly rental rate
- Term of lease
- Responsibilities for repair, maintenance, and upkeep
- Sublet and assignment

- Pets, smoking, cleanliness
- Permissible property uses
- House rules (noise, parking, number of occupants)

The option part of the contract gives you the right to buy the property at some future date. As a minimum, the option should include

- The amount of your option payment
- Your purchase price for the property
- The date on which the purchase option expires
- Right of assignment
- The amount of the rent credits that will count toward the purchase price of the house

Tenant Buyers - Benefits

Lease qualifications

Qualifying for a lease option may be no more difficult than qualifying for a lease (sometimes easier). Generally, your credit and employment record need meet only minimum standards. Most property owners will not place your financial life under a magnifying glass, as would a mortgage lender.

Low initial investment

Your initial investment to get into a lease option agreement can be as little as one month's rent and a security deposit of a similar amount. At the outside, move-in cash rarely exceeds $5,000 to $10,000, although I did see a home lease optioned at a price of $1.5 million, which asked for $50,000 up front.

Saving forcibly

The lease option contract typically forces you to save for the down payment required when you exercise your option to buy. Often, lease options charge above-market rental rates and then credit perhaps 50 percent of your rent toward the down payment. The exact amount is negotiable. And once you have committed yourself to buying, you should find it easier to cut other spending and place more money toward your house account.

Fixed selling price

Your option should set a firm-selling price for the home, or it should include a formula (perhaps a slight inflation-adjustment factor) that can be used to calculate a firm price. Shop carefully, negotiate wisely, and when you exercise your option in one to three years (or whenever); your home's market value could exceed its option price.

If your home has appreciated (or you've created value through improvements—see below), you may be able to borrow nearly all the money you need to close the sale.

100% financing

You also can reduce the amount of cash investment you will need to close your purchase in another way: Lease-option a property that you can profitably improve through repairs, renovation, or cosmetics. After increasing the home's value, you may be able to borrow nearly all the money you need to exercise your option to buy the property.

For example, assume that your lease option purchase price is $75,000. Say by the end of one year, your rent credits equal $2,500. You now owe the sellers $72,500.

Through repairs, fix-up work, and redecorating, you have increased the property's value by $10,000. Your home should now be worth around $85,000. If you have paid your bills on time during the previous year, you should be able to locate a lender who will finance your purchase with the full $72,500 you need to pay off the sellers. Or, as another possibility, you could sell the property, pay the sellers $72,500 and use your remaining $12,500 in cash proceeds from the sale to buy another property.

Reestablishing credit

A lease option also can help you buy when you need time to build or reestablish a solid credit record. Judy and Paul Davis wanted to buy a home before prices or interest rates in their area rose above their reach. But the Davis's needed time to clear up credit problems created by too much borrowing and Judy's layoff. The lease option proved to be the possibility that helped the Davis's achieve their goal of home ownership.

Investors – benefits

Although the lease option might help you buy a property, it can also prove to be a good way for you to rent out your investment property. You can structure lease options in many ways. This type of agreement can typically benefit you as an investor in at least three ways:

- lower risk,

- higher rents, and

- guaranteed profits

Finding Lease-Option Buyers and Sellers

To drive the best bargain on a lease option as a buyer/lessee, don't limit your search to sellers who advertise lease options. These sellers are trying to retail their properties. It will be tougher for you to find a bargain here. Instead, look for motivated for-sale-by-owner sellers in the "Homes for Sale" classified ads.

Or, you might also try property owners who are running "House for Rent" ads. Often, the best lease-option sellers will not have considered the idea until you suggest it. When you search for tenant-buyers, generally you will be able to choose from three different classified newspaper ad categories:

- Homes for sale,

- Homes for rent, and

- The specific category "lease option" that some newspapers include

Unfortunately, no one can say which ad category will work best in your market. Experiment with each of these choices. To learn which one is pulling the best responses, ask your callers to tell you in which category they saw the ad. Don't simply assume that any single category listing will draw the largest number of qualified callers.

Lease options for investors – a good start

To start building wealth fast without investing much money up front, look at the following example:

While searching for the ideal career, Jane was also looking for a place to live. So, she located a lovely but dilapidated apartment house. The building was making a painful transition from rentals to condominiums. Units were for sale or rent. But sales were practically nonexistent. With her head held high, preliminary plans and a budget tucked under her arm, and she decided to make the manager an offer he couldn't refuse.

She told him that in lieu of paying the $800-a-month rent that was being asked for a 2-bedroom, 2-bath unit, she would renovate the entire apartment. Then she agreed to spend $9,600 for labor and materials, the equivalent of a full year of rent payments. Along with a 12-month lease, she also requested an option to buy the unit at its $45,000 asking price.

Three months later, Jane was on her way. She then bought her renovated condo unit at her lease-option price of $40,000. Then, simultaneously, sold the unit to a buyer for $85,000. After accounting for renovation expenses, closing costs, and Realtor's commission, she netted $23,000.

Jane no longer had a home, but she had found a career. Twenty years, 23 homes, and 71 properties later, Jane had become not just independently wealthy, but a recognized entrepreneur.

The Lease-Option fix

The lease-option fixture truly magnifies your profit potential. Instead of buying a property outright, you find motivated sellers who are willing to lease-option their property to you at both a bargain rental rate and a bargain price. Typically, such sellers were not advertising their property as a lease option. They generally are trying to sell it. In fact, they may not even have thought of the lease-option idea until you put a proposal in front of them.

Controlling without Cash

Ideally, through this lease option, you gain control of the property for two to five years. Your cash-out-of-pocket totals less than you probably would have paid in closing costs had you immediately bought and financed the property with a new mortgage.

Next, you spend some money on spruce-up expenses (if desirable) and re-advertise the property as a lease option. You find tenant-buyers and sign them up on a lease option with you as the lessor. Your tenant-buyers agree to pay you a higher monthly rental and a higher option price than you've negotiated for yourself in your role as lessee with the property owners. You profit from the markup in price and option money.

Your rate of return skyrockets because you gain control of a property with almost no cash investment. The up-front money you've collected from your tenant-buyers more than covers the amount you paid as option money to the property owners. Essentially, you're buying wholesale and selling retail—without actually having to pay for your inventory.

Does the Lease-Option fix works for everyone?

Theoretically, it can work. (Just make sure you protect yourself fully in the lease-option contracts you sign). Personally, I wouldn't try it. For my taste, giving someone an option to buy a property that I don't yet own seems fraught with dangers. Nevertheless, in theory this technique can yield high returns.

Lease-Purchase Agreements

As a practical matter, the lease-purchase agreement works about the same as a lease option. However, instead of gaining the right to either accept or reject a property, the lease-purchaser commits to buying it. As an investor, you can often persuade reluctant sellers to accept your lease-purchase offer, even though they may shy away from a lease option.

The lease-purchase offer seems much more definite because you are saying that you will buy the property—you would just like to defer closing until some future date (say, six months to five years more or less) that works for you and the sellers.

It just looks as if it is working

I say "as if" it is working because there is a loophole. You can (and should) write an escape clause into your purchase offer called "liquidated damages." With a liquidated damages clause, the sellers could not sue you to go through with your purchase (specific performance) if you chose to back out.

Nor could they sue you for money damages that they may have suffered due to your failure to buy. Instead, the liquidated damage clause simply permits your sellers to pocket your earnest money deposit. In effect, your earnest money really acts like an option payment. No matter what the purchase contract appears to say, in reality you have not firmly committed to buy.

Amount of the Earnest Money Deposit

The real firmness of either a lease-option or a lease-purchase contract lies in the amount of the up-front money the seller receives—regardless of whether it's called an "option" fee or an "earnest money" deposit.

If you want to really show a seller that you intend to complete a lease option or a lease-purchase transaction, put a larger amount of cash on the table. By the same token, if you truly do want to "keep your options open," negotiate the smallest "walkaway" fee that you can, even if it means conceding elsewhere in the agreement.

Contingency Clauses

You also can escape from your obligation to buy a property through the use of contingency clauses. If the contingency (property condition, ability to obtain financing, lawyer approval, sale of another property, etc.) isn't met, you can walk away from a purchase and at the same time rightfully demand the return of your earnest money or option fee.

Master-Lease an Apartment Building

To make money in real estate, you need to control a property. The most common way to obtain this control is through ownership. Some investors, though, don't buy their multiunit properties—at least not right away.

Instead, they master-lease them. As we just discussed, buyers and sellers typically use a lease-option agreement to convey condominiums and single-family homes. But to acquire (without purchase) apartment buildings, you would use a master lease.

A Turnaround Property

Say you locate a 12-unit apartment building that is poorly managed and needs upgrading. You might offer to buy the property. But you really don't have the financial power to arrange new financing, and the owner doesn't want to sell the property using a land contract or purchase money mortgage. Currently, the property barely produces enough cash flow to pay expenses, property taxes, and mortgage payments.

The owner wants to turn this money pit into a moneymaker, but lacks the will to invest time, effort, money, and talent.

The solution: master-lease the entire building and guarantee the owner a steady no-hassle monthly income. In return, you obtain the right to upgrade the building and manage the property to increase its net operating income.

Generally, a master lease gives you possession of the property for a period of 3 to 15 years and an option to buy at a prearranged price. During the period of your lease, you would pocket the difference between what you pay to operate the property, including lease payments to the owner, and the amounts you collect from the individual tenants who live in each of the apartments.

This technique resembles the lease-option sandwich that we discussed earlier, only it applies to multiple-unit buildings as opposed to single-family houses.

Achieving Turnaround

- Upgrade the property and implement a thorough maintenance program;

- Your more attractive property and more attentive management will attract and retain high-quality tenants;

- Meter the apartment units individually to reduce utilities;

- Raise rents to reflect the more appealing condition of the property and the more pleasant ambiance created by the new higher-quality, neighbor-considerate, rule-abiding tenants;

- Shop for lower-cost property and liability insurance coverage; and

- Reduce turnover and encourage word-of-mouth tenant referrals to eliminate most advertising expenses.

Not only did this turnaround increase the property's net income, but, correspondingly, the higher net income, lower risk, and more attractive apartments lifted the value of the building. This means that when you exercise your option to buy, you will be able to arrange 100 percent financing to pay off the owner, yet still give the lender a 70 to 80 percent loan-to-value ratio as measured against the property's new higher value.

Sell Your Lease-Option Rights

Instead of going through with your purchase of master-leased property, you might sell your leasehold and option rights to another investor. Given the much higher net income that you've created, you can assign your rights at a very good price markup.

In effect, an investor would pay for the right to earn more per year as the master lessee, before tax cash flow (plus future rent increases) for the remaining term of the master lease. He would also gain the right to buy the property at a now bargain price.

CHAPTER 10

GAINING MAXIMUM FROM YOUR INVESTMENT

In real estate—unlike the stock market—you not only make money when you sell; you can make money when you buy. In the stock market, you cannot buy a stock for less than its market value. In real estate, these transactions occur every day.

Market value versus property value

To see why you can buy properties for less than they are worth, you need to delve into the meaning of the term "market value." Under market value conditions, a property sale meets the following criteria:

- Buyers and sellers are naturally motivated.

- Buyers and sellers are well informed and knowledgeable about the property and the market.

- The marketing period and sales promotion efforts are sufficient to reasonably inform potential buyers of the property's availability (no forced or rushed sales).

- There are no special terms of financing (e.g., very low down payment, reduced price, below-market interest rate).

- No out-of-the-ordinary sales concessions are made by either the seller or the buyer (for instance, sellers are not permitted to stay in the house rent-free for three to six months until their under-construction new house is completed).

As you think through this description of market value, you will realize that owners who are in a hurry to sell may have to accept a price lower than market value. Likewise, an owner-seller who doesn't know how to market and promote a property will not likely receive top dollar.

Or, say, the sellers live out of town and don't have accurate information about recent sales prices. Or maybe the sellers don't realize that their property (or the neighborhood) is ripe for profitable improvement. In general, we can place those owners who will sell at a bargain price into eight categories.

Distressed Owners

Every day property owners hit hard times. They are laid off from their jobs, file for divorce, suffer accidents or illness, experience setbacks in their business, and run into a freight train of other problems. Any or all of these calamities can create financial distress. For many of these people, their only way out of a jam is to raise cash.

If that means selling their property for "less than it's worth," then that's what they're willing to do.

For these people are not just selling a property, they are buying relief. Under these circumstances, as long as the sellers believe they have gained more from the sale than they've lost, it's a win-win agreement for both parties. If you are willing to help people cope with a predicament—as opposed to taking advantage of them—seek out distressed owners. On occasion, they will give you the bargain price (or favorable terms) you want.

Real Estate Investment Tag Line

Real estate gurus say that you make money in this business when you are buying. This also means that you have to learn the ways to buy property only at a price and time that will give you the advantage. You must therefore, know

- Where to buy

- When to buy

- From who to buy

Where to Buy Real Estate Property

Buy subject to existing financier

There are times when property can be bought from other buyers when it is still under the financier. Although it sounds complicated and even illegal, it is pretty simple and straightforward. Subject to simply means that the property is subject to an existing mortgage, which is already in place on that property. This means that the terms that the lender created remain the same including the name the loan was purchased in. In this case, the terms you agree with the seller are between you and them; you are not assuming the loan. All you have to do is to ensure that you follow the terms of the existing loan.

So what about the "due on sale" clause?

Many investors (not sellers) often have concerns about the due on sale clause when they use the subject to method. So what is the due on sale clause and what does it state? This simply states that the lender has the right to call the entire note if the terms that were on the initial agreement are not fulfilled like payments being made or even the transfer of the deed being done without the full payment of the original loan.

Keep in mind that the lender's job is not collecting payments. Their job is to give loans at a fairly higher interest rate than what they are paying; they make profits from the difference. If no payments are being made, and the loan is categorized as a nonperforming one, then it is only fair for them to foreclose to recapture that property and sell it again. Every buyer and seller is definitely worried about what would happen if a loan is called due. But if you think about it, the lender also has a lot to lose when the loan is called due.

For starters, if a lending institution takes back property, they are sort of "punished" by the federal government because they have a nonperforming loan. Well, this is what is called bad debt. When this happens, the government puts limits such that the lender cannot lend eight times the amount of bad debt. So if a bad debt is $100,000, the lender is restricted from lending $800,000.

Property sold through the subject to method is often pretty much discounted. The seller is probably someone in some financial distress looking for someone to bail them out like someone who wants to downsize after a divorce, or is moving states. You have to be careful before you commit your resources and ensure that the fancier, usually a bank, has not started foreclosure process on the property.

Owner sales

Sometimes property owners want to dispose off their property without incurring agent costs. Such property can be acquired at greatly discounted prices since the owner does not incur much expense in the process of selling. You can access such property easily by looking around as you move, reading newspapers, and even ads on the internet. The classic hand-written rectangular signs that read: "for sale" are common in many neighborhoods.

Bank owned properties

Bank-owned-properties, also commonly referred to as REOs are a great to acquire property at discounted prices. Usually, when banks reacquire property, they are more willing to dispose it so that they get rid of the loans from their accounting books; remember the penalties we talked about in the subject to approach. Take advantage and negotiate for a good price.

Add to notes

Owner Financing

Some property owners opt to advance financing and take over the property ownership until buyers are able to complete purchase.

The owner may try out several income deals with the property including leasing it, renting it or just holding it. In the meantime, the owner may sell a note and transfer ownership to another owner. It is a great way to generate reasonable income if you have the means to finance such property.

As a seller if you are ignorant

Some sellers underprice their properties because they don't know the recent prices at which similar properties have been selling. I confess that as a seller, I have made this mistake of selling too low because I was ignorant of the market.

In one particular case, look at this person living in Palo Alto, California. The rental house he decided to sell was located in Dallas, Texas. A year earlier, the house had been appraised for $110,000, which at the time of the appraisal was about right. So he decided to ask $125,000. He figured that price was high enough to account for inflation and still leave room for negotiating.

The first weekend the house went on the market; three offers came in right at the asking price. Immediately, of course, he knew he had underpriced. What he didn't know but soon learned was that during the year he had been away, home prices in that Dallas neighborhood had jumped 30 percent. After learning of his igno-rance, he could have rejected all the offers and raised the price. Or he could have put the buyers into a "bidding war."

But he didn't. He just decided to sell to the person with the cleanest offer (no contingencies). He thought he was making a good profit; why get greedy?

Due diligence – keep it straight

Although good deals go fast, don't jump in before you've checked to see whether there's water in the pool. Always remember that not all bargain priced properties represent good deals. You have scored a good deal only if you can sell the property for substan-tially more than you have put into it.

Beware of underestimating fix-up expenses. Beware of hidden defects. Beware of environmental problems (e.g., lead paint, un-derground oil storage tanks, asbestos, contaminated well water). Beware of pouring so much cash into improvements that you'll have to overshoot the rent level that tenants are willing and able to pay.

Always temper your eagerness to buy a bargain-priced prop-erty with a thorough physical, financial, market, and legal analysis. Especially in cases of low- or nothing-down seller financing, many beginning investors grab at a "great" deal without first putting it under a magnifying glass. Act quickly when you must. But the less you know about a property, the greater your risk.

The seller's disclosure statement

Most states now require certain types of sellers to complete a disclosure statement that lists and explains all known problems or defects that may plague a property. But even if your state doesn't yet mandate seller disclosure, you still should obtain a disclosure form (most major realty firms keep blank copies on hand) and ask the owners to fill it out.

In reviewing a completed disclosure statement, however, keep in mind the following five trouble points:

- Sellers are not required to disclose facts or conditions of which they are unaware.

- Disclosure reveals the past. It does not guarantee the future. By completing the statement, sellers do not warrant the condition of the property.

- Many disclosure questions require somewhat subjective answers. Are playing children a neighborhood "noise" problem? Is a planned street widening an "adverse" condition?

- Disclosure statements may not require sellers to disclose property defects that are readily observable.

- Pay close attention to any owner (or agent) statements that begin, "I believe," "I think," "as far as we know," and other similar hedges. Don't accept these answers as conclusive. Follow up with further inquiry or inspection.

Seller disclosure statements help alert you to potential problems. But even so, independently check out the property to satisfy yourself that you really know what you are buying.

Finding sellers – going all out strategy

The networking way

Check out what is happening in your network. Attend seminars, events and a host of other activities to promote what you have. What's surprising, though, is that so few buyers and sellers consciously try to discover each other through informal contacts among friends, family, relatives, coworkers, church groups, clubs, business associates, customers, parent-teacher groups, and other types of acquaintances.

So don't keep your search a secret. Tell everyone you know. Describe what you're looking for. Why search alone when you can enlist hundreds of others?

What else can you do?

- Advertise "I buy properties" in the real estate classifieds.

- Advertise on your car or truck with a magnetic "I buy properties" sign.

- Make your car or truck a mobile billboard. Paint it with an "I buy houses" advertising message.

- Mail out "I buy houses" postcards to owners in your farm area.

- Mail out "I buy houses" postcards or letters to owners who are being foreclosed. Advertise your property needs to real estate agents. Contact attorneys (real estate, divorce, bankruptcy, estate, tax

- Contact yard care companies that maintain properties for lenders after the owners have abandoned them.

- Network with friends, family, acquaintances.

- Agree to pay bird-dog fees to anyone who refers you to a great buy.

- Approach other investors who have just bought a property at a foreclosure sale. They may be willing to quick-flip for a small profit.

- The power of internet and social media – Create accounts on social media sites, promote what you have. Write blogs, white papers and informative books to promote yourself. Have a website of your own and run ads wherever necessary.

Boosting your property value

You're now well on your way to create instant wealth. Before the sharp interiors can woo your prospective tenants, you must get them to keep their appointments to inspect the homes that you are offering. Nothing will accomplish this goal better than a striking appeal.

The striking appeal

You can write an award-winning newspaper ad that will make your phone ring. But your Madison Avenue talents will fall flat when great tenants pull up in front of the building and immediately begin to ask themselves, "What are we doing here? This place is nothing like I imagined. Do you think we should go in?

The place your live – upkeep regularly

More than likely, hundreds (maybe thousands) of people will pass by your property each week. What will they notice about the property? Those flower gardens and brick walkways seem to reach out and invite us to come inside." If you want your building to generate more income, create an inviting exterior.

Create award-winning publicity with knockout curb appeal. Not only will an attractive, well-kept exterior appeal to a better class of tenants, it will also increase tenant satisfaction and reduce turnover. To create strikingly attractive appeal, try making these improvements:

Clean up the grounds and other common areas

When you first take over a property, get busy with a meticulous cleanup of the grounds, parking area, and walkways. Pick up trash, accumulated leaves, and fallen tree branches. Build a fence to block that view of the dumpsters. Tell tenants to remove their inoperable cars from the parking lots, parking spaces, or driveways. If abandoned cars are parked on the street, ask the city government to post them and tow them.

Yard care and landscaping

Tenants and homebuyers alike love a manicured lawn, flower-lined walkways, mulched shrubs, and flower gardens. With landscaping, you can turn an ordinary building into a showcase property. With landscaping, you can create privacy, manufacture a gorgeous view looking out from the inside of the units, or eliminate an ugly view.

Especially if you're looking at a holding period of three to five years (or longer), put in those small plants, shrubs, flower gardens, and hedges now. When you sell, those mature plantings will easily earn you a return of at least $10 for each $1 the landscaping cost you.

Common areas - Sidewalks, walkways, and parking areas

Replace or repair major cracks and buckling that may appear in your sidewalks and parking areas. Remove all grass or weeds growing through the cracks. Edge all of the areas where the yard abuts concrete or asphalt. Neatness pays. Overgrown grass and weeds really stain the curb appeal of a rental property— precisely because these types of blemishes signal that the property is a rental.

Fences, lampposts, and mailboxes

For purposes of good looks, privacy, and security, quality fencing can enhance the value of a property. Just as certainly, a rusted, rotted, or tumbledown fence blemishes the property; likewise, rusty lampposts with broken glass light fixtures. For a nice decorative touch, add a white picket fence or a low stone fence in the front of the building. If the building houses a cluster of mailboxes make sure the mail area is kept neat and the mailbox lobby or porch area present a good first impression.

The facade and exterior of the building

Now, turn your attention to the exterior of the building itself. The building must signal to prospective tenants that you take good care of your property. Paint where necessary or desirable. Repair wood rot. Clean roof and gutters.

Next, imagine ways to enhance the building's appearance with shutters, flower boxes, a dramatic front door and entryway, and new (or additional) windows. Can you add contrasting color for trim or accent the building design with architectural details? How well does (or could) the property's exterior distinguish it from other comparably priced rental properties?

CHAPTER 11

THE MISTAKES IN REAL ESTATE INVESING

When boarding on a real estate investment project, there are abundant financial and tax issues considerations to address. Below is a specimen of issues to consider as you plan your project.

Debt and Equity Financing

- Sources of debt financing range from commercial banks and life insurance companies to public entities.

- Critical to the project financing is whether the debt will be recourse debt or nonrecourse debt

- Generally, all debt will require "bad boy" provisions, which requires guarantees for unprofessional acts.

- Guarantees on debt (recourse) are more likely to be required for more highly leveraged projects, and more speculative projects.

- An owner's goal is to minimize debt guarantees other than the bad boy provisions

- Equity can come in many forms, including "sweat equity", such as deferring development fees, leasing fees, or loan guarantees.

- Equity can also come from donating appreciated property to the development activity.

- Cash equity is typically needed for most projects.

Deal Structuring

- Most real estate is held, for tax purposes, in single purpose partnership form – either Limited Partnerships or Limited Liability Companies.

- The financial terms of a deal between partners can be as varied as you can imagine, and will be respected as long as the deal meets the IRS criteria of "Substantial Economic Effect".

- Many real estate projects have different return on investment terms for cash investors vs. the developer/ operators.

  o For cash investors, they potentially receive a preferred cash return of x% on their invested $'s, with the developer/operator receiving a greater portion of the profits above the chosen x%. Internal Rate of Return computations are frequently invoked here.

o Also, cash investors often receive their invested $'s returned before the developer/operator receives their sweat equity return, especially if the developer/operator receives an enhanced return. This preferential treatment is used to align incentives, as well as to defer the taxation on the value of sweat equity until turned into cash.

Tax Considerations of Operations

• The goal of many real estate investments is to distribute cash from the partnership to the investors that is greater than the taxable income distributed

• This can be accomplished through enhanced depreciation deductions, generated by:

• Cost segregation studies.

• Careful review of capitalization vs. expense for repair and maintenance expenditures.

- Understanding and negotiating the terms of leases that are favorable to landlord.

- For investors, our experience is that they desire two things – cash distributions that meet projections, and timely K-1's for their personal tax return reporting requirements.

- Many projects refinance and increase their debt on properties in order to receive a return of their capital while retaining ownership of the property. Thus, they often times will have ownership of the property without any net cash invested in the project after the refinancing. This refinancing and distribution can typically be completed on a tax deferred basis, and is an attractive alternative to sale of the project.

Tax Considerations on Disposition

- Because of the enhanced depreciation deductions taken on properties, the sale of property can leave the investor with taxable income greater than the cash they receive on sale.

- Thus, many owners will attempt to structure as per the prevailing norms like exchange on the disposition of property.

- This requires many legal steps to be taken, but essentially requires all cash that is received on sale to be reinvested in another property within a defined time period.

- Property can also be disposed of by contributing it to another partnership in exchange for partnership units.

CHAPTER 12

EFFECTIVE STRATEGIES – ONLINE AND WEBSITES

Internet and Your Business

The market often quotes statistics related to consumer behavior in residential real estate as more than 70% - no one underestimates the impact of the Internet on a broker's business anymore. Your office with the address end in ".com" has already become the most-visited of all your offices.

You should ensure that your best office is staffed with the best people, and that it receives your full attention and resources. Employing new online marketing strategies and lead conversion tactics is critical to getting customers through the door and keeping them coming back.

Cultivating prospects to closed transactions can take several months, so leveraging your automated online office and content is a must for your business success and agent productivity.

Internet and Real Estate Data Availability

The value chain of servicing real estate customers classically includes marketing the home and obtaining consumers, in addition to providing access to product, expert advice and transactional services. The widespread obtainability of digitized real estate data and content has opened this formerly industry-controlled value chain to new companies and business models.

Given that data distribution costs on the Internet are low and the new online consumer is hungry for information, brokers should now be focusing on how to competently leverage all their data for maximum business benefit rather than limit consumer access to information.

The wide distribution of massive amounts of raw data has just begun, and the pace will only accelerate: the next task is to offer home buyers and sellers' meaningful tools that help them navigate the home purchase or sale process with a real estate professional.

Brokers should carefully evaluate their data acquisition strategy in the midst of all these changes.

Internet and Attracting Customers Online

Typical paid online customer acquisition is focused on paid advertising using search engines, listing portals, various media sites and lead generation companies. Brokers should pay more attention to their online product/content syndication and acquisition   strategies; leveraging real estate data offers an attractive customer acquisition opportunity.

In competitive markets the cost of data goes towards marginal cost, so you may not want to buy   basic content, but rather, leverage data and its presentation abilities from others. Selectively syndicating your own proprietary content out to others might be the most cost-efficient customer acquisition option ever.

The Importance of an Online Presence

The online real estate office is representative of both your corporate positioning and your sales office— and it is now visited by the majority of your prospective and existing customers, potential new agents and even possible investors. However, attracting and retaining your customers at your online office is just the beginning.

Your online office is also a highly productive customer management tool where prospects and existing customers interact on a continual basis. If one presumes that the average home sale cycle ranges from 6-18 months, the only way to cost-efficiently capitalize on these online consumers for such an extended time frame is to apply technologies such as interactive Web site tools populated with fresh, relevant content, evaluate and segment prospects and maintain an ongoing dialogue and relationship until the transaction is closed—with minimum manual effort.

Underscoring the value of a robust online strategy in real estate is the fact that the market is evolving at a record pace. New entrants are entering the industry almost daily—powered by the potential of the Internet.

These new entrants are utilizing new technologies and have open access to massive amounts of information. Brokers and agents alike are now faced with an abundance of new opportunity and competitive threats.

The Real Estate Value Chain

The residential real estate value chain consists of roughly four steps,

- Marketing/customer acquisition

- Access to product

- Expert advice

- Transaction-related services

The emergence of the Internet triggered a shift in marketing strategy as agents and brokers began to create and publish Web sites designed to promote themselves and acquire customers online. Next, it became possible to provide online "access to product" or simply "access to for sale listings" through the creation of IDX and VOW data feeds and direct data feeds from the MLS.

This change was motivated by a mixture of evolving consumer behavior and real estate professionals' interest in less expensive means to market real estate, coupled with a more efficient solution to provide enhanced brokerage services.

Data Access

The current trend toward transparency and open access to data—and the resulting debate about such open access—is now gradually affecting the expert advice portion of the real estate value chain. Traditionally, some real estate professionals have viewed property data protection as a method of justifying the "expert advice" they provide clients, much in the same way that access to listings—or lack of it—has in the past been believed to be necessary to ensure consumers make contact with a real estate agent.

However, past history through decades of human communication has proven that information which is not deemed confidential or proprietary will eventually become publicly available. If you don't agree with this premise, then consider the following select facts:

- Search Google for "home valuation" and get 1,510,000 search results. Free, instant, automated valuations (or price predictions) are available through a handful of real estate sites.

- Sales comparable options from public records, sometimes and sometimes even from the MLS are   available online through dozens of free Web sites—from broker sites to hobbyist sites to lead generation services.

- For sale property listings are available through tens of thousands of sites, some more accurate than others.

- School data and other neighborhood data are available through practically every large broker site.

As an Agent Select the Following Options

- Protect and hide my real estate data because my services will somehow be devalued by consumers as they access more data themselves.

- Enable consumer access to real estate data and find ways to leverage this access to maximize my own business, e.g., allow me to provide more quality advice to educated consumers and be more productive and efficient in servicing customers while increasing the volume of consumers with whom I can do business.

Option one is a non-option. If it holds true that a professional adds no value, a devaluation would happen regardless of efforts to "hide" data that is not completely confidential or proprietary.

It is clear that option two is the option brokers and agents should support. In the end, access to more data will inevitably be made available to the consumer, and there is little that can be done to change this fact. A true professional service provider will always be valued as the "expert advisor," particularly when he or she is facilitating easy access to more information.

The fact is that home purchase decisions are not simple; the entire process requires complex judgment and the presentation of subjective variables that cannot be effectively delivered through machines or technology only.

Real Estate Data acquisition

Real estate listings are not the only type of data real estate professionals should take into consideration. Given that there are millions of information-hungry consumers to satisfy, the acquisition and distribution of raw data has only just begun. The good news is that the cost of non-proprietary and non-confidential data in a competitive market goes towards its marginal cost, which is nearly zero online.

This means it is now far easier for companies to acquire this raw data at low or no cost, and then transfer one's true competitive differentiation to much higher-margin, valued-added services.

The challenge is how to format volumes of data into a presentation or user interface that makes sense and is appealing to end users. Consumers are ultimately interested in value-added content and presentation, not just the raw data packaged into a mediocre user interface.

With the wide availability of data now on the Internet, the true value in the delivery of real estate brokerage services occurs in the display and analysis of data and related content.

Those brokers and agents who endorse open data access and transparency with the consumer should have a clear idea in their mind of how they would answer the following questions:

- What kind of data do I want to offer and display to my users?

- Do I have the resources to continuously package, display and analyze raw data or should I let others do that given the increased pace of innovation online?

- Where can I get this data/content? Is someone able and willing to syndicate it for my use or does it need to be purchased?

- If I get the content for free, is there a downside or cost/risk in using it?

Your Website

To acquire customers online, real estate professionals typically work with—or advertise at—the following types of online sites:

- Lead generation companies, through which brokers or agents can buy home buyer or seller leads (i.e., not online visitors to your own site, but actual   customer prospects).

- Real estate media sites, which offer consumers interesting content around which real estate professionals can buy advertising such as banners.

- Listing portals, where you can promote your listings for a fee.

- Search engines, e.g., the horizontal ones like MSN, Google and Yahoo where you can receive free "organic" traffic through search results and/or pay for additional enhanced advertising.

The ultimate goal of a sound online customer acquisition strategy is to spend the least amount of advertising dollars necessary to reach the most qualified consumers through the most effective, efficient media—ensuring that this media fulfills its promises and supports the listing broker business model. The two most interesting strategies of customer acquisition outside of the typical "paid advertisements" are:

- Superior product that generates significant word-of-mouth and PR effects.

- Selective content syndication to drive traffic back to your Web site.

Getting back customers online

Customer acquisition to your online office doorstep is just the beginning. The next step is to offer consumers information and a user experience that (1) keeps them coming back and (2) allows them to easily register/form a business relationship with your company.

Today's online consumer has been spoiled with an overall superior user experience in other industry verticals and they are used to instant gratification. That means forcing consumers to register personal information with no immediate benefit to them is unlikely to yield positive results. Optimally, you would allow consumers to interact with your service without any hurdles or barriers and make it easy to request more information and/or register or contact an agent—at any point in the process.

CHAPTER 13

REAL ESTATE SELLERS – ALL YOU SHOULD KNOW

You could use the following strategies while representing sellers of the residential real estate.

Discover & Defeat Potential Pitfalls Up Front

Upon Retention, ask your client pertinent information and take immediate action, such as amending or cancelling the contract within the attorney review provision:

Client's Marital Status

Clients in divorce proceedings often assume their soon to-be ex-spouse does not need to be involved in the real estate sale of their principal residence. Until divorce proceedings are final, regardless of whether only one spouse is a title-holding spouse, Illinois law requires the signature of both spouses to effectively release, waive or convey a homestead interest.

Mortgages, home equity loans and lines of credit

Find out about all loans your client has on the property and the approximate balances. Before the attorney approval expires, calculate whether or not there are adequate sale proceeds to pay off all loans/liens as well as all other anticipated closing costs.

Insufficient Sale Proceeds

Does your client require sale proceeds to purchase other real estate? How much money is required? Will a post-closing possession escrow or tax re-proration escrow for their sale tie up funds they require for their purchase?

Any Existing or Potential Foreclosure

Is the property in foreclosure or has the Seller defaulted on their mortgage(s)?

Leases, Tenants, Rentals

Are there any rentals, leases or tenants at the property (don't overlook rental of parking spaces)? What are the terms? Is the Buyer willing to take the property subject to the leases/ tenancies?

Pending Lawsuits or Judgments

Are there lawsuits or other judgments against your client or the property? Find out now to allow yourself time to clear the defects without having to delay closing.

Verify warranties & representations

Verify warranties and representations your Selling client made in the contract and revise as necessary during attorney review

Is your client aware of:

- Government violation notices concerning the property;

- Notices concerning any increase in property taxes or property assessments;

- A pending re-zoning of the property; d. Boundary line disputes over the property;

- A pending condemnation or Eminent Domain proceeding;

- An easement(s) on the property not shown on public record;

- Hazardous waste on the real estate; h. Improvements or upgrades to the property not included in the most recent tax assessment;

- Improvements to the real estate which may be eligible for the home improvement tax exemption;

- Whether or municipal permits were properly obtained for any improvements made to the property.

Research Property Tax Issues

Negotiate a more accurate tax proration. File for any exemptions to which your client is entitled. Ensure your client receives monies from the County to which they may be entitled for unfiled exemptions, appeals or certificates of error which are not yet concluded. Rather than speculating or employing customarily used tax prorations, instead:

Research the Property's Information with the County Assessor for

- Exemptions filed or not filed. Have your client file for exemptions for the most recent and previous tax years for which they are eligible but failed to file. For example, in Cook County they may file up to the past 4 tax years for the homeowner's exemption if they can prove eligibility;

- Assessed value increases or decreases (compare to the prior year's assessed value and calculate the percentage of increase/decrease);

- Any improvements not yet assessed;

- Any certificates of error filed or not yet concluded, or assisting your client in filing a certificate of error as appropriate;

- Any appeals not yet concluded.

Make a Phone Call to the Township Assessor

Ask what he/she believes the percentage of increase for the next tax bill will be for that particular property. If not ascertainable, then ask whether or not the local municipality's recent decisions will cause an increase or decrease property taxes for that tax year.

Place the Onus on the Buyer

Place the onus on the buyer to Obtain Lender Approval of Credits from Seller to Buyer, rather than trying to salvage the deal at the closing table when the buyer's end lender first learns about and disapproves the credit. Via the attorney review provision, make credits from Seller to Buyer contingent upon Buyer having disclosed the credit, in writing within X business days, to the end lender (not simply the mortgage broker).

Provide that if the lender disapproves of the credit, then Buyer's failure to proceed with the transaction based upon the same shall be deemed a default.

Duty to Update Statutory Disclosures

Inform your client that during the pendency of the contract, they have a duty to update the Residential Real Property Disclosure Report. E.g. if the property floods after disclosures are signed but before possession is delivered, then the form must be amended and re-signed by the parties.

Do not Outright Agree to a Vague Request

Do not agree for an Appraisal Contingency allowing Buyer to cancel if the property appraises at a value lower than the purchase price. Instead, CLARIFY the terms:

- Whose appraisal? The Buyer's/ Lender's appraisal report, and not an outside report (e.g. Buyer decides mid-way to forego financing and pay cash, and then wants to cancel based on an independent report obtained by Buyer individually).

- When can the Buyer cancel? Recommended: the same date as the mortgage contingency deadline.

- Is the Seller entitled to a copy of the appraisal report? Require that Buyer, within a specified time, notify Seller in writing that the property did not appraise out and produce a written copy of Lender's Appraisal Report.

- Is the Buyer required to appeal? If so, what will be the time frame? Recommendation: Buyer has three (3) business days do the following:

- Formally challenge and/or appeal the lender's appraisal results (comparable or "comps" found by the appraiser), and

- Request the Listing and/or Selling Agents research and produce documentation of more accurate comparable property sales ("comps") to the buyer's lender, and c) if lender allows, request and pay for the lender to obtain a second appraisal.

• Can Seller Offer a Price Reduction? Require that, if the appraisal appeal is not successful, then Buyer must allow Seller the opportunity within a specified time frame to offer to reduce the purchase price as an alternative to Buyer's outright cancellation. If Seller makes a timely written offer to Buyer to reduce the purchase price to the lender's appraised value, then Buyer will be obligated to proceed with the transaction.

In the following chapter, we will give you a rundown of all of the things you need to take into account when you are considering flipping houses. This covers your process from start to finish in easy to understand terms that won't baffle you, but will leave you with a definite impression of what successful flipping is all about.

CHAPTER 14

BONUS REAL ESTATE INVESTMENT STRATEGIES

Here is a list of other real estate investment strategies you can try out if the ones listed above are not exactly your thing.

Real Estate Wholesaling

Find great real estate deals, craft a contract for them and sell. That's how simple this investment strategy is. It is one of the most attractive for newbies who may not have enough equity to purchase properties directly. Such contracts are bought by real buyers who also pay you handsomely, not only for the labor of crafting the contract but also for being the one to have located the property. Such deals are known to fetch up to $5000. Sometimes, you could make a lot more. It is the size of the deal (the amounts involved) that determine how much you make as a real estate wholesaler.

The wholesaler is ideally a middleman who links the actual buyer and the actual seller.

Wholesaling is particularly attractive to starters because it is said to be possible to start, even with zero capital.

NB: Like everything else worth trying on the investment market, wholesaling is not easy either. It is not an easy achievement to realize because building a reliable network in real estate is quite hard. However, it is doable; since others have done it and succeeded.

The secret in wholesaling lies in ensuring that you cast your nets further afield. You could start with nothing but still make it in real estate. It's going to take a lot of dedication, though, to reach your peak.

Turn Key Properties

Turnkey properties refer to the real estate options that come ready for renting. Many turn Key properties are made of fairly lower priced materials. Some are mobile homes discussed earlier. Many of these come with tenants already. This means that you can begin financing your investment sources and loans as soon as the property becomes yours legally. They are attractive because they require little extra input from you after you execute the purchase.

Turn Key properties often sell from $35000 to $150000. It is always good to seek a buying price that is as low as possible to be able to rake in returns as soon as possible. In fact, since many Turn Key properties only provide middle level rentals, it is not a good idea to allow you too much freedom of spending on them. If you overspend on Turn Keys, you may not achieve your financial objectives in good time to meet obligations such as repaying loans. If you buy them within reasonable range, Turn Key properties are great sources for maintaining cash flow. As mentioned earlier, if you are a foreigner, Turn Key properties are great for foreigners who may not be provided with the larger equity required for investment in other types of real estate that require a significant amount of cash.

Owing to the fact that Turn Key properties are regarded as lower range investment types, they are also prone to lots of manipulation and possible unorthodox practices. You must therefore practice due diligence if and when you want to purchase.

Due Diligence Practices That Keep You on the Safer Side of the Transaction

Note that although these practices and precautions are meant to help you acquire your Turn Key property safely, they are also true in other types of real estate transactions. They will help you carry on with minimized risk.

i. Ensure that you get references for any company you decide to deal with.

ii. Confirm the actual value of the property. It is prudent to invest in a property appraiser. Remember that Turn Key properties have a relatively thin margin of profitable returns. Therefore, you must get your facts right before you purchase one.

iii. It is also helpful to check the background of the property manager you wish to deploy.

iv. Trace the track record of the company you are dealing with. You can find out whether the company has a presence online. If it is online, check out the reviews about their services.

v. Seek details of the details of the property you intend to purchase

Find out the state of the following

- The furnace

- Water heater

- Air conditioner

- Electrical installation

- Plumbing system

You should also find out how reliable the projections for returns are. Even turnkey properties may have long periods of nonoccupancy and/or even need significant maintenance that may cost substantial amounts of money.

Mobile Home Parks

Mobile homes parks are usually set on private and public parks. You can buy off the whole park if they are set on a private park. Once you have the title, you can resell it or undertake an even more dynamic business venture by taking advantage of the variety of tenant types you can rent the homes to. This variety gives leverage over risks too. The cash flow from such property is reasonable and can be used to finance future investments.

RV Parks

You can also buy a park and rent it out to motorized homeowners. This is a great way to make modest income with little input, especially if you have inherited a park but you cannot quite put up any income generating structures on it. Another advantage with this type of real estate investment is that you can easily opt out. Your tenants are highly mobile and if you seal the right contracts for their occupation, they will give you room when you need it. You can start your own mobile home or set up equally good income generating structures.

Hotels and Motels

This type of investment can be a cash machine especially in tourist rich locations. You can rent out rooms on such property at premium prices. If the property is large enough, it can provide sufficient income to balance out the low seasons too.

The down side of such an investment is that, relying on tourists and visitors is a risky venture. If the tourists don't turn up or the economy plunges, it could be a real economic disaster. Properties that rely on visitors and tourists are subject to many fluctuations. There will be times when you will not have sufficient visitors to meet the running costs. When the latter happens, you can easily experience a cash flow crunch.

Purchase in cash and resell on contract

If you can assemble sufficient start up resources, you can take advantage of the market with people who cannot raise mortgage loans by intervening with contract sale of property. You can purchase properties and resell to those who are interested but cannot get proper financing to own such property immediately. Once you resell such property, of course at a much higher price and interest, make sure that you collect a huge down payment from the buyer. This method is an advantage to you because you can hold the property for as long as you want and transfer ownership at your convenient time. The new owner then acquires the right to collect rent or lease payments from the long-term buyer.

CHAPTER 15

THE OVERALL FLIPPING PROCESS

You may think by now that you have a good idea of what it's all about, but it's a complex business and you need a little handholding to start off with. Research the geographical area where you are thinking of buying houses. See what the market is like. Are houses selling relatively quickly? What kind of houses are selling and to whom? This gives you an idea of who you can market your finished properties to, but it also gives you an idea of the kind of houses to look out for. You won't have much joy buying up houses split into bedsits or small studios if your market is the family market. You may find the studios a good investment if you are in an area where rental property is scarce and there are a lot of single students looking for such accommodation. You may even find it beneficial to talk to the accommodations office of the local University to find out if there is a need for more accommodation. They may well be able to find you renters or they may even have the funds to purchase suitable rental accommodation blocks or houses once they meet their standards.

Never buy blind. Always be aware of what the renovation costs are likely to be and don't underestimate them. You need to add together the price of the house and the estimated cost of repairs and see if you could sell a house for much more than that. If you can't then the price is too high or it's too much of a risk. In country areas, find out if a home meets current code for:

- Electricity

- Plumbing

- Asbestos

- Footings

- Roofing

- Rot

These are all potential expensive items to deal with so always look at the structure of the home and if you decide that a deal looks good, sign on condition that inspector's reports are satisfactory. If you find out too late, you could find that it takes a long time to get the house up to code and all the time the house is yours, you are paying out for the privilege of owning the house.

Schedule your works and tie contractors down to working a set schedule. First fix, which is wiring within walls or laying plumbing pipes should always be dealt with before you even think of finishes. Then installation of plumbing fittings such as toilets, baths and showers need to be complete before tiling can be done. Kitchen units need to be fixed so that a plumber can do a last fix on electrical installations such as dishwasher, waste disposal etc. The order of the work is essential and any holdups will cost you money. In particular in a rural area, find out what the restrictions are and the regulations stipulate the disposal of waste, via a septic tank. If the current tank does not meet code, this can be a very costly renovation job to have to do.

The works should begin as soon as you own a house. Thus planning during the legal phase is vital to save you time. Hire a skip so that rubbish can be placed into it to get the home cleared out and ready for work. These are placed on the street in front of the house and may need booking in advance, so make sure this kind of detail is dealt with.

Do deal with suppliers

You need to know that you can obtain discounts in different stores. The things you will have to buy will include kitchen cabinetry, worktops, island furniture, lighting, drywall, cement where necessary, tiling and flooring. Get yourself in a position where you have accounts set up so that when you take possession of the house, you are able to order in advance and be sure that everything you want is delivered at a discount price.

If suppliers think that you are going to give them regular business, they will be more inclined to give you better discounts. Shop around. Some suppliers will be less expensive than others, but look for quality. People have been shortchanged for so long now that they are very savvy when it comes to quality. A quality home will sell better than one that has been thrown together quickly for a profit. You are no longer in a world where people are gullible enough to buy the property based on what someone says about the quality of fittings. They want to see them, touch them, feel the quality, so don't kid yourself that using cheap fittings will help you achieve more profit. It's more likely to result in more complaints and that doesn't help your reputation.

Visit real estate agents. Find out the kind of properties that are selling well in the area where you are thinking of investing. Let them know you are in the market for buying houses which are offered at great prices and get your name known to local sales offices as well as using information they give you to help you decide your market.

Above all else, target your market. If the area is one which is commonly occupied by executives and single working people, they want their homes to be impressive because these are people who are much more likely to socialize and want to impress their friends and colleagues. If the house you buy is meant for families, then they are not that interested in the number of walk in closets and are more inclined to look at what you provide in the way of a utility room, mud room, play room and children's bedrooms and whether the area offers great schools within an easy reach. They will also want to know that the area is safe for kids and you need to bear all of these things in mind when buying a property. You need to do a lot of homework to make this business a success. Never buy a property just because you think it's cheap. You may not be comparing it realistically with other properties in the area and from area to area – the price differences are staggering.

Do all of your homework and know exactly what it is you intend to do and how you will finance the whole project. Set a budget. Know you have available funds. Work out your costings and make sure that you have a contingency or a little money left over to cover unexpected items. Then know what your competition is like because when people look for houses, they want to buy what they see as the best value for money. That's what you are aiming on providing them with and that should always be your aim. If you pay too much or overplay the renovations and it costs you more than anticipated, your eventual sale will give you less profit.

By doing your homework, you can save a lot of money on renovations, on improving the quality of the property and on marketing the home at the end of the work. Get a great real estate agent on your side and you really can make a killing. Make sure that the real estate agent offers great advertising and good quality photographs and description and never be afraid to say if you feel that any of the work they are doing isn't up to scratch. A kind word about the quality of images may be all it needs to change what potential buyers see. Bad photos don't do a house justice. Don't be afraid to follow up when you go to sell the house because it's your responsibility right up until the moment the purchaser signs on the dotted line.

The Flipping Rule 70%

There is something called the flipping rule in the real estate investment market. Ideally, when flipping, you are required to push your way to reducing the buying price of property to 70% of its current value. This should exclude the repair costs. For example, if the house is presently worth $200k, and your assessment of the repair costs come to $10k, in proper flipping, it would be 70/100x200K=140k-10k= $130k

The flipping process then begins with the repairs and makeovers. You would consequently repair the house with 10k and resell it at the current value = $200k.

From the above calculations, it is evident that you would make away with a significant gain from the deal.

The secret behind success in flipping requires acting with great speed. The idea is to resell the house as soon as possible at its current value since the future is not always guaranteed. Moreover, sealing the flipping deal and process fast ensures that you avoid incurring unnecessary losses in

- Possible taxes
- Monthly bills such as charges for financing
- Condo fees in applicable situations
- Maintenance costs etc

It therefore follows that flipping is an active engagement and not a passive income strategy.

Common Reasons for Flipping

Flipping is commonly used by experienced investors to finance daily activities in business. It can also be used to fund passive income investments when and where need be.

A word of warning

If you are thinking of buying outside of your area or even in a foreign country, be aware that rules may be different and that you need to investigate what rules are applicable in the area in question. I remember one person who tried to invest abroad, not being aware that the homes he invested in were unable to be let. These were in a residential area away from the usual tourist route and he thought he could make a fortune renting to holidaymakers. He didn't know the local tradesmen and it cost him a fortune to get the houses up to scratch and was then told that he couldn't rent them anyway!

This may be a big investment, but at least go in with your eyes open and know what you are getting yourself into. This book should have you covered and was written by someone who flips homes regularly and who knows how important it is to be realistic in your approach at all stages of the game.

If you do take note of these warnings, you can find a lot of property at great prices and use your expertise and contacts to update those homes either for the rental market in your area or for resale. Either way, do your math and check out the market before investing because when you do that, you take less risk and are more likely to be able to start making a living with your investment in bricks and mortar.

CHAPTER 16

HOW TO CREATE A REAL ESTATE BUSINESS PLAN

Since we have severally emphasized the need to devise an investment plan before you venture, here are the highlights that you need to include in your investment plan. You have learnt the ropes and the tricks in real estate investment; you probably learnt to move to the next level by committing your funds into property. Use the investment plan below to chart out a clear path for your investment.

If you took some time and swept a glance across your environment, you will begin to appreciate the value of a plan. A plan is like a road map to a destination. One of the common but costly mistakes that many beginner investors make is to start off in real estate investment and without a plan, then go on to figure out what they need to do after they have made strong commitments. This terrible mistake leads to investment disasters more often than not.

It can be compared to setting out on a journey without knowing how to get to your destination. If you are going to a place, you have never been, it is important to seek direction. You will then either get a map to, or of the place you wish to visit, or carry your GPRS gadget or Smartphone to assist you reach there. In short, it is foolish to venture in real estate investment without carefully planning.

The Content of an Investment Plan

Mission Statement

A mission statement is an expression of your purpose. It also highlights the benefits you wish to get from venturing in real estate investment. It is important to craft such a statement so that you align all your activities along that mission and vision. In fact, the words mission and vision are frequently used in mission statements to capture the essence of a venture. Ideally, a mission statement should answer the "why" question. It tells you why you are doing what you are doing in the first place.

Goals

When crafting a real estate business plan, you need to clarify your goals. Before you take off, you must know where you are going. Otherwise, you will hover and make cyclic movements that end nowhere.

- You must clearly state what you want to get from your real estate venture and what time you estimate it would take you to accomplish your goals. Setting timeframes for achieving the goals helps you to set out on a program.

- You need to be specific when stating your goals. If you intend to build a business empire worth $20 million, make sure that you write that down. If you wish to raise funds to buy larger commercial properties, state it and the amount it should cost.

- You should also split your goals into short and long-term ones so that you can assess your progress in the pursuit of the long-term goals. Short term goals also help to motivate you in an otherwise seemingly huge and intimidating mission. When you see the small bits you have already accomplished, you acquire the synergy to go on with your mission. You should also take cognizance of the fact that your plans, as well thought out, as they may seem now, may be altered by external factors. Do not over worry when such an eventuality comes around. Adjust as necessary and move on with the larger picture.

- Strategize. We have looked at the many strategies you can employ in your situation to gain advantage in real estate investment. These strategies are selective. Not all strategies will work for everybody. Therefore, you need to select the strategies that fit your investment option. Choose a strategy that best serves you with the least inconvenience and risk. Pick a customizable strategy. It could be flipping, single-family investment for rental returns or note selling. Just make sure that you write the strategy down to pursue a clear course of action to achieve your objectives and final goals.

- Note that there may be some aspect or aspects of your plan, which seem vague. Do not be worried with such encounters. If anything, no one knows everything. You will discover that some of the details will become clearer down the investment road. Once you take active steps to execute your investment plan, you stumble upon more information you can fill in the gaps with. Take courage and ask any experts or authorities in your area of interest. Sometimes what seems strange and mysterious only takes a phone call to resolve.

- Set realistic timeframes for achieving your goals. Indeed, it is critical to set timeframes for all activities you need to engage in to realize aspects of your goals. Do not be overambitious with the timelines. You should consider all factors and risks that may slow you down. This is the way to be realistic and move at a comfortable pace that does not burn you out. Unrealistic timeframes and objectives turn out as unachievable and begin to frustrate you and everybody else you have lined up to play a part in the pursuit of your investment goals.

- Figure out criteria that the deals must meet if you are going to invest in a given niche. For example, it is critical to consider such aspects as

  - Value of your investment loan

  - Cash flow

  - Your upper seal on the purchase/s you intend to make

  - Repair and makeover costs

  - The time frame for accomplishing the repairs and other fixes

  - The location of your chosen investment option etc

Setting criteria is critical because it keeps you focused on what you want. You will be able to brush aside the many possible temptations you are likely to encounter in your investment pursuits. A criterion also helps you stick to your budget, hence remaining realistic. A criterion is the one element you earnestly require in order to exclude emotion from your investment decisions.

Deriving a criterion that your investment should meet within a given period and environment will help you avoid kissing frogs. You can tell when you see them. You do not have to go deep to sense the discrepancy. In other words, you can easily detect any deals that won't work for you.

- Draw a marketing plan. There is no point making an investment, which won't be attracting income. You should be proactive in your investment plan and figure out how you will attract sellers and possible buyers /tenants at the end of the process. Think of where and how you can strike the best deals. Some of the options available in modern day include online searches, MLS agents, and direct mail.

- Financing. This is the backbone of your plans. Figure out your best but most affordable financiers. Decide whether you will use a bank loan or cash. Consider the effectiveness of equity partners such as mortgage merchants, seller-financing agencies or even lease properties available. Experience shows that source financing can be a long winding path. If you are in a position to secure private money, it is always the best option. It can expedite your investment program. This quality could be critical as markets often fluctuate unpredictably. Learn how to be in good books with private money sources.

- Craft the details of the deals. Ensure that you lay out every step in each of the deals you wish to execute step by step. Detail every step in the process of buying and selling at a profit.

  - List all income sources

  - Write down all the expenses including the possible "surprise" expenses

- You must also figure out how you can exit when things do not turn out as you expect. This is commonly referred to as an exit plan (find out more about how to develop a comprehensive exit plan here). In fact, an exit plan is an essential part of your real estate investment plan. Your exit plan must be clear. Craft a backup plan that could include some of the following alternatives.

  - Selling a note

  - Flipping

  - Leasing

  - Bird dogging

  - Selling a title holder identity

  - Renting

  - Holding etc

The whole point behind exit plans is that you should try to visualize how the end of your investment looks like. You should factor in possible pitfalls and what you can do in case the worst comes to that.

- Paint out the future picture of your investment option look at the ideal scenario in 10 years. Try to show the bugs, the projected cash flow, sales expectations, trades, cash with cash returns etc.

NB: You must have noticed by now that this aspect of your business planning renders many similarities with the goal setting we highlighted earlier in the plan. However, a closer look should tell you that this is a more visual impression of what you want to put on the ground. It includes details that goals cannot possibly have. Whereas goals are more like a wish list, this part of the planning is a vision of where you are going. You can actually see what you are driving at in color and structure concretely.

You do not want to incur losses or be stuck in a bad business relationship. Whereas an exit plan in your business plan is an essential part of your personal planning process and decision-making, you should pay special attention to the contracts you get into to include a clear exit plan that does not commit your time or finances unnecessarily.

- Flexibility: Your investment plan must have a level of flexibility to cater for the unforeseen aspects in the process. Flexibility allows you to devise alternative options for your project. If you cannot find what you seek, feel at liberty to change your strategy or even markets.

- Set systems and teams. You must figure out all the members of a team that will help you achieve your investment objectives. As we mentioned in an earlier chapter, you need people with an array of expertise and skills. It is hard to succeed in real estate as a lone ranger. Draw a list of people you will need to accomplish the short-term objectives and the long-term ones. Those who help you achieve your short term objectives may also become long-term business associates to take up future ad hoc activities related to their skills. You will need people from all skills categories in the real estate industry. You need to have some lawyers you will consult on legal matters, all across to cleaners to spruce up your premises after a repair or makeover. It is of critical importance to outline clear roles for each of your team members. It should also be clear who oversees the various processes and who issues direction in relation to particular aspects. In the end, you should make some brief computations that illustrate what it would take to have every one of your team members on board.

- Finances. You should describe your financial position at the point you decide to venture in real estate investment. You should clearly state

    - What you have now

    - What you expect to have in a given time frame

    - Potential pitfalls

You should also update your financial position as it changes over time and realign your goals and objectives according to the dictates of your situation. Make sure that your financial information is clear to you before you begin to make any commitments.

Summary

Whereas it is imperative to craft a business plan using the highlights given here, you should always bear in mind that a business plan is meant to be a guide, not a rule. Do not remain rigid even where there are roadblocks. If you set out to travel to a given location using road "A", you certainly wish to get there with this route because it is fairly understood. However, if bridges are swept away by floods, yet you still have to get there, you might be forced to take road B or C; a flight or use an alternative route. Sometimes the alternative route may be even shorter than you knew. At other times, many times, the alternative routes present unforeseen challenges, which may make your mission a little tricky. Adaptability is an essential quality in business pursuits.

Feel free to change some aspects of your plan and take the next best route if you foresee huddles down the road. This does not mean that you are wrongly deviating from your well thought out plan. This is called adaptability. In fact, being rigid is not part of investment planning. There are forces that are outside your scope and control even at the point of planning. Such forces are the ones that may force you to alter some aspects of your plan. You will consequently drop some aspects even as you embrace new ones. The most important element in any unfolding events that require such adjustments is to keep your eyes on the goals you set and keep evaluating your performance and asking whether you are still on course.

The point is made with planning. Just remember that failing to plan, is planning to fail.

CONCLUSION

I want to thank you once again for downloading this eBook and I sincerely hope you had a good read.

The book aimed at giving you a true insight into the world of real estate investments, and hopefully you are well versed with the real estate market by now.

The industry welcomes everybody and provides all with an equal chance at making a profit.

But it will require a little intelligence and the knack to identify and grab the opportunity to land a lucrative deal.

In chapter 1, we started by discussing where you should start as you begin your real estate investment venture. The chapter was aimed at helping you to open your eyes to the possibility that everything in your target market is constantly changing.

Chapter 2 explained the need to select a niche in the market that you want to serve. Don't just assume that you can do anything and succeed especially because success comes after carefully analyzing your niche and preparing a business plan for your real estate investment business.

Chapter 3 introduced some five ways in which you can deal with your property. The chapter also stressed on the importance of bargaining and why you must consider it as the top most aspect to consider.

Chapter 4 focused on the various aspects of the property that you must consider, before you make an investment. Investing in property should always be compared to investing in jewelry and just like how you would consider the design, price and value, you have to do the same with the property.

In chapter 5, we read about the 5 types of sales that you can take part in, to find your properties. These are always subject to availability and given the amount of homes that get built and sold these days you will always have one available at close intervals.

Chapter 6 spoke of the types of investments that you can make, in terms of the type of ownership. It is apparent from it that you need not always be the sole investor and can find someone, who will be interested in sharing the costs with you. The chapter also has some additional mistakes that you must avoid while in the real estate business.

And then we looked at the 5 things that you must be wary of, when you are investing in real estate. You have to develop patience and also inculcate the habit of doing extensive research, before you make an investment.

Chapter 8 is an updated version of my previous book which carries information and strategies related to current trends. You can use these ideas with full faith as they have been written out of the years of experience I have

Chapter 9 is very interesting for me as I was able to convey golden principles that serve as a guideline for anyone who is in the real estate business. Especially if you are new in this field this chapter will be very much useful for you.

Chapter 10 has thought provoking strategies that will help you to gain maximum money from the investments you have made. I have not hidden any ideas to myself but tried to give everything, so that as a reader you gain more from what is said.

Chapter 11 clearly talks about what should not be done if you are in the business of Real Estate. Most of the books today focus on the best things said about the industry, but I wanted the readers to also understand the negative aspects of the business.

Chapter 12 is clearly the game changer in the recent times, particularly in the Real Estate industry. If you have a presence online, you have every chance of growing your business exponentially. You have multiple avenues to make your presence felt online and people can see you all the time.

Chapter 13 is some useful tips that all of you at some point of time might miss out. These are crucial at the time of closing a particular deal or especially when you are considering to take a decision when you are all by yourself.

Chapter 14 is a new chapter I added in the new edition to discuss some additional strategies that you can implement in your real estate business to make more money. Some of the strategies we discussed include real estate wholesaling, turnkey properties and others.

In chapter 15, we discussed the overall flipping process and how you should work around with costs and market price to come up with an offer for the purchase of any property.

Then came chapter 16, which essentially introduces the importance of a business plan for your real estate business and how to prepare one for your business.

I have made sure that this book is updated with latest trends in the Real Estate industry for you take maximum out of it. This book is a sincere effort of mine, to get close to reality and not to hide anything from you as a reader. Upon reading, you will understand that I have stressed more on the industry insights which others may find it as a top secret.

With the efforts put into writing this book, I hope to have shared at least a few of the best tips, which will get you started off on the right foot.

Here's to wishing you luck with all your real estate ventures. Happy reading.

Good luck!

FUNDAMENTALS OF SUCCESS-FUL THINKING

Free Bonus "<u>Instant Access</u>" Click Below For Your Bonus: https://success321.leadpages.co/fundamentals-of-successful-thinking/

.

Made in the USA
Middletown, DE
02 September 2016